Swedenborg

BUDDHA
of the
NORTH

T0124895

Swedenborg
BUDDHA
of the
NORTH

D. T. Suzuki

Translated and with an Introduction by Andrew Bernstein
Afterword by David Loy

**SWEDENBORG
FOUNDATION**
West Chester, Pennsylvania

Reprinted without changes 2019.

Suedenborugu was first published by Heigosha, Tokyo, Japan, 1913.
"Suedenborugu: Sono Tenkai to Tarikikan" (Swedenborg's View of Heaven and 'Other-Power') was first published in *Chûgai Nippô*, February 1924.
Translations by Andrew Bernstein, 1996.
Introduction by Andrew Bernstein was first published as "D. T. Suzuki and Swedenborg" in *Arcana* 1, no. 4 (Summer 1995): 5–19. Reprinted by permission of author. "The Dharma of Emanuel Swedenborg: A Buddhist Perspective" was first published in *Arcana* 2, no. 1 (Fall 1995). Reprinted by permission of author.

Swedenborg Studies is a scholarly monograph series published by the Swedenborg Foundation. The primary purpose of the series is to make materials available for understanding the life and thought of Emanuel Swedenborg (1688–1772) and the impact that his thought has had on others. The Foundation undertakes to publish original studies and English translations of such studies and to republish primary sources that are otherwise difficult to access. Proposals should be sent to: Editor, Swedenborg Studies, Swedenborg Foundation, 320 North Church Street, West Chester, PA 19380.

Library of Congress Cataloging-in-Publication Data

Suzuki, Daisetz Teitaro, 1870–1966.
  [Suedenborugu. English]
Swedenborg : buddha of the north / D. T. Suzuki ; translated by Andrew Bernstein.
     p.   cm. — (Swedenborg studies ; no. 5)
  Includes bibliographical references and index.
  ISBN 0-87785-184-0 (paper); 0-87785-185-9 (cloth)
    1. Swedenborg, Emanuel, 1688–1772. 2. Mystics—Sweden—Biography. I. Title.
II. Series.
BX8748.S8813 1996
198'.5—dc20
[B]   95–46033 CIP

Photo credits: D. T. Suzuki, in Cambridge, MA, 1958, p. 2; and D. T. Suzuki, at Matsugaoka Bunko (Pine Hill Library), Kita-Kamakura, Japan, 1963, p. 76: original photographs by Francis Haar, reproduced by permission of Tom Haar, Tom Haar Photography, Honolulu.

Edited by Mary Lou Bertucci
Interior layout by Joanna V. Hill
Typeset in Sabon and Gill Sans by Ruttle, Shaw & Wetherill, Inc

Swedenborg Foundation
320 North Church Street
West Chester, PA 19380
www.swedenborg.com

Contents

A way stands open into heaven,
but none can enter the way
except those who have heaven within them.
—Emanuel Swedenborg
Conjugial Love, para. 500

The Way is near.
—Dozaikin

Zen calligraphy by Jiun, 1718-1804

Foreword

by Tatsuya Nagashima

Daisetsu Teitarô Suzuki was an internationally known Buddhist scholar whose fame comes not only from his voluminous works on Buddhism written in Japanese but also from his popularity as a Buddhist teacher who wrote in English. Today, most libraries in the world have some of Suzuki's English-language books about Zen and Mahâyâna Buddhism.

I knew the writings of D.T. Suzuki long before I discovered those of Emanuel Swedenborg. I had bought Suzuki's newly reprinted thirty-two-volume complete works in 1980 because I then thought that Zen Buddhism could provide Japanese Christians with insights for spiritual growth. I was surprised to learn, however, that this devoted Buddhist had translated Christian theological works, and not only one book but four by the same author—Emanuel Swedenborg.

Born in 1870, a Buddhist physician's fourth son, Teitarô Suzuki was first influenced by Zen teachings in high school. But it was at the age of 20 that Suzuki first practiced Zen at the well-known Kokutaiji Zen temple in Toyama. The following year he studied under the Zen Master Imakita Kôsen at Engakuji Temple and later, after Kôsen's death, under the Zen Master Shaku Sôen. It was Sôen who gave Teitarô the name *Daisetsu* (literally, "a great simplicity"), upon the completion of his Zen training. After his Zen studies, Suzuki matriculated at Tokyo University, majoring in philosophy.

After leaving Tokyo University in 1895, Suzuki published his first book *Shin Shûkyô Ron* (A New Interpretation of Religion), in which he presents the idea of universal truth and the importance of religion (any religion) in setting out this truth for humanity:

> I am convinced that religion itself depends on a free response from a human being, and it rules over innumerable behaviors of men and women since it is the basic principle of human life. . . . Human minds are never healthy without religious belief, and human cultures are not perfect without religion. Further, religious faith and scientific progress can certainly go hand in hand.[1]

In this short work (only 147 pages), Suzuki rejects the idea of a deistic universe in which a detached God sits and looks at his handiwork from the outside. Indeed, Suzuki prefers the term "Truth" to "God," as a closer representation of the concept of Great Wisdom. He also asserts, with other Buddhist scholars, that the universe, in terms of its totality, has neither cause nor effect. The earth turns by its own power; plants grow and perish by themselves. Life is *a priori* and not a created force. Suzuki views this Buddhist pantheism as preferable to Christian monotheism, since Christianity adds another mysterious being of "God" to the already given mystery of "Universe." Despite the fact that, at this time in his life, Suzuki's idea of Christianity was restricted to the stereotypical image of modern evangelical Protestantism, he believes that religion, under any denomination, is important to mankind:

> I do not want to employ any sectarian names such as Buddhism, Christianity, Islam, and so on; but I would rather employ the term *religion* instead, because my insistence is not simply on the doctrines of any single religious sect but on religion itself. . . .

The essence of religion is that people know the Great Mercy
and its Truth therewith, and apply them to their daily life. . . .
The totality of religion is Truth. . . . Truth existed long before
Jesus Christ or Buddha was born [but] both founders perceived Truth and proclaimed it to the world.[2]

It is interesting that, this early in his career, Suzuki was writing ideas similar to those espoused by Swedenborg, who also
wrote about a universal church in which all religions are included as far as they believe in one God and shun evils. Yet, at
this time, Suzuki was probably not familiar with Swedenborg's
writings, since he first encountered the Swedish mystic's works
when he lived in the United States between 1897 and 1908.
During that time he worked as an editor for the Open Court
Publishing Company, under the leadership of the American
scholar Paul Carus, who was a proponent of Monism or the
"science of religion."[3]

In 1907, while still living in the United States, Suzuki met
Beatrice Lane, a Boston native who had studied at both Rad-
cliffe College and Columbia University under such teachers as
William James, Josiah Royce, and George Santayana. Doubtless, Lane was familiar with the writings of Swedenborg
through her studies in philosophy and religion (William
James's father, Henry James, Sr., was a well-known reader of
Swedenborg). Moreover, on Quincy Street in Boston stands
the Swedenborg Chapel, where for many years the influential
Swedenborgian minister William Worcester was a driving
force behind the congregation. It may be that Lane con-
tributed to Suzuki's interest in Swedenborg's writings. Suzuki
and Lane married in Japan in 1911. After their marriage, Lane
became a Buddhist scholar herself, publishing *The Shingon
School of Mahâyâna Buddhism* in 1931. Looking back over
his married years, Suzuki wrote:

Since the beginning of our married life, mutual commitment was focused on the proclamation of Eastern thoughts to the Western people. We had no other joy and happiness than to promote, by our own [possible] endeavors, this communicative understanding between East and West.

However, speaking from our own feelings, we could have communicated only between us in person about what we think on religious issues without a special regard to an external influence. But both of us have been led in this direction guided by some sort of destiny.[4]

Suzuki returned to Japan in 1909, where he became a lecturer in English at Gakushûin and Tokyo University, specializing in William Blake, a writer heavily influenced by Swedenborg's writings. In 1910, he published *Tenkai to Jigoku* (Heaven and Hell) as the first Japanese translation of Swedenborg's theological works from an English edition. During this same year, Suzuki attended the International Swedenborg Congress in London and served as a vice-president. But the years 1913–1915 saw Suzuki intensify his study of Swedenborg: in 1913, he wrote *Suedenborugu*; in 1914, he translated *The New Jerusalem and Its Heavenly Doctrine* into Japanese *(Shin Erusaremu to Sono Kyôsetsu)*, followed by the translations of *Divine Love and Wisdom (Shinchi to Shin'ai)* in 1914 and *Divine Providence (Shinryo Ron)* in 1915. This period of Swedenborg studies was followed by a nine-year interval of silence on the subject, until Suzuki published a nine-page article about Swedenborg in 1924. In this short essay entitled "Swedenborg's View of Heaven and 'Other Power'" *("Suedenborugu: Sono Tenkai to Tarikikan")* [see Bernstein introduction, n. 8], Suzuki explains heavenly innocence and the angelic acknowledgment that all good emanates from God. Other Swedenborgian concepts such as "correspondence," "free will," and "equilibrium" are also discussed. After this publication, Suzuki is silent (at least publicly) about Swedenborg.

The question of whether Suzuki ever considered or wrote about Swedenborg after the 1920s intrigues Swedenborg scholars, although the majority of Suzuki scholars find the Swedish mystic's influence to be relegated to Suzuki's midlife. Still, pieces of the puzzle may be missing; although Suzuki's collected Japanese works consists of thirty-two volumes, Suzuki wrote a number of works in English, many of which have not yet been published in Japanese. All of his works, on subjects ranging from Zen Buddhism to various schools of Mahâyâna Buddhism, are evidence of the Buddhist scholar's lifelong search for *satori* (enlightenment). Certainly, we are reminded of what Suzuki himself wrote about Swedenborg in *Suedenborugu*: "[His] 84 years of life were totally devoted to science and religion." And Suzuki's 96 years of life were also devoted to religion, a kindred spirit over time and space.

There is, however, one Suzuki scholar who feels that Swedenborg's influence on the Japanese scholar may have gone farther than previously acknowledged. In a memorial essay on Suzuki, Kiyoto Furuno wrote:

> I read *Suedenborugu* written by Suzuki, and I had an impression from it that Suzuki was a Swedenborgian. It is quite true that Zen Buddhism was first introduced around the world by Suzuki, but it is also true that Swedenborg was first introduced to Japan by him. . . . I have a conjecture that [Suzuki's] basic thought was more or less influenced by Swedenborg. It seems to me that Suzuki was able to translate Zen Buddhism into English with such insight and clarity because Suzuki's brain had previously been trained by Swedenborg's mysticism in his younger years.[5]

As the first translator and publisher of Swedenborg's original Latin texts into modern Japanese, I understand the difficulty involved in the translator's craft. Andrew Bernstein's translation of *Suedenborugu* and *"Suedenborugu: Sono*

Tenkai to Tarikikan" takes Suzuki's classic-styled Japanese and renders it into modern English. I am happy that now an excellent English translation of Suzuki's seminal work is available for English-speaking Swedenborgians and scholars.

Notes

1. D.T. Suzuki, *Suzuki Daisetsu Zenshû* (Collected Works of Daisetz Suzuki), vol. 23, ed. Shôkin Furuta (Tokyo: Iwanami Publishing Company, 1982), 13. All translations into English are done by the author of this foreword.

2. Ibid., 57–58.

3. It is possible that Suzuki first became aware of Swedenborg from the World Parliament of Religions, held in Chicago in 1893; he was a translator for Shaku Sôen. The Parliament was initiated by Swedenborgian lawyer Charles Carroll Bonney, who gave its opening address; six Swedenborgians also gave addresses at plenary sessions. See L.P. Mercer, ed., *The New Jerusalem in the World's Religions Congresses of 1893* (Chicago: Western New Church Union, 1894). Bonney and Carus cooperated in efforts to follow up on the Parliament, and Bonney's article "Genesis of the World's Religious Congresses of 1893" was published in *The Monist*.

4. D.T. Suzuki, *Suzuki Daisetsu: Hito to Shisô* (Daisetsu Suzuki: His Person and His Thoughts), ed. S. Hisamatsu, S. Yamaguchi, and S. Furuta (Tokyo: Iwanami Publishing Company, 1972), 182.

5. Ibid., 80-81.

Preface

by Andrew Bernstein

I began translating these works by D.T. Suzuki two years ago
at the request of Leonard Fox of the Swedenborg Association.
At the time, I was apprehensive about the task: I had already
done work on Suzuki in my studies in Japanese religious history, but was unfamiliar with Emanuel Swedenborg or with
Suzuki's interest in him. As I delved into the project, I became
more intrigued with both Swedenborg and the young Suzuki
who so admired him.

Suzuki's Japanese presented a special challenge. Written in
the first decades of the 20th century, *Suedenborugu* and *"Suedenborugu: Sono Tenkai to Tarikikan"* use classical grammar
and diction that make reading difficult for someone more familiar with current Japanese usage. I have tried to render as
faithful a translation as possible, although any translation is
inevitably an act of personal interpretation. The works translated here can be found in *Suzuki Daisetsu Zenshû,* the 32-
volume set of Suzuki's collected works.

The problems of translation became especially clear to me
when I tried to put back into English Swedenborg's passages
that Suzuki had translated into Japanese. Suzuki based his renditions of Swedenborg's works on English translations of the
original Latin. Although Suzuki never directly cited these
translations, I was usually able to locate English versions that
so closely mirrored Suzuki's Japanese that I take them to be his

sources. However, this was complicated by the fact that Suzuki's renditions sometimes differed from standard English translation of Swedenborg's works, as published by the Swedenborg Foundation. Discrepancies between the Japanese and the standard English are cited in the notes. Another standard reference used for letters and reminiscences is the three-volume *Documents concerning the Life and Character of Emanuel Swedenborg*, ed. R.L. Tafel (London: Swedenborg Society, 1875–1877).

This project could not have been completed without the help of many people. Special thanks goes to Keith Vincent and Zenno Yasushi, who spent long hours helping me untangle Suzuki's Japanese. I am also grateful to Wayne Yokoyama, Nagashima Tatsuya,* and Kohso Iwasaburo, as well as Robert Sharf, Roger Corless, and Kirita Kiyohide for their assistance. Swedenborgian scholars Donald L. Rose, George F. Dole, William R. Woofenden, and Leonard Fox helped in verifying my notes on Swedenborg, often locating Suzuki's English sources when I had difficulty. Indeed, this project would not have been undertaken without the impetus of Leonard Fox, who has helped in more ways than I can cite here. Thanks also goes to Mary Lou Bertucci, who shepherded my work through the publishing process. And, finally, thanks to my family and friends for standing by me in this and everything I do.

---

*In the preface, introduction, and endnotes to the Suzuki translation, the traditional Japanese order of family name followed by a given name has been used.

Introduction

by Andrew Bernstein

In the summer of 1954, while meeting with religion scholars Henry Corbin and Mircea Eliade, D.T. Suzuki was asked what resemblances he found between Mahâyâna Buddhism and the theology of Emanuel Swedenborg. According to Corbin, Suzuki suddenly brandished a spoon and declared, "This spoon *now* exists in Paradise. . . . We are *now* in Heaven." During the ensuing conversation, Suzuki went on to say that Swedenborg was "your Buddha of the North."[1]

Why did Suzuki, a man largely responsible for making "Zen" into a household word, equate Swedenborg, an eighteenth-century Swedish scientist turned mystic, with a Buddha? Looking through Suzuki's writings of the 1950s and 1960s, one finds only a few other references to Swedenborg. For example, in an essay dating around 1950,[2] Suzuki states simply that "Swedenborg's doctrine of correspondence holds good in Buddhism too."[3] Unfortunately, Suzuki does not elaborate on this doctrine, mentioning it only in passing.

Another quick reference to Swedenborg appears in a 1960 talk entitled, "Zen and Philosophy." Here, Suzuki says that the world of Zen is not philosophical but poetic, and later notes that the same holds true for the "New Jerusalem," a spiritual era that Swedenborg said had already begun in the spiritual world and was about to begin in our own. Suzuki further explains that this world of poetry is not to be confused with mere "lies," that it should not be seen as a realm completely disjointed from the mundane.[4]

But once again Suzuki's citation of Swedenborg serves only as a brief example and is incidental to the argument as a whole. Indeed, in a book where Swedenborg could have figured quite largely, *Mysticism: Christian and Buddhist* (1957), Suzuki mentions him only once. He writes in an appendix that the Buddhist teaching of transmigration, which is based on the premise of ethical retribution, "reminds us of Swedenborg's doctrine of correspondence, according to which things on earth have corresponding things in heaven or hell."[5] The bulk of the book, however, is devoted to a Buddhist interpretation of Meister Eckhart, the medieval Dominican mystic.

Why is so little space devoted to the "Buddha of the North" in Suzuki's later writings, and particularly in a book that deals with Christian mysticism?[6] After all, between 1910 and 1915, Suzuki had translated four major works by Swedenborg and had also written the small book on Swedenborg's life and thought, *Suedenborugu*, that is here translated into English.[7] Furthermore, his 1924 essay, "Swedenborg's View of Heaven and 'Other-Power,'"[8] concludes, "There is a great deal I wish to write concerning Swedenborg, but that remains for another day."[9]

That day never came, but it is obvious from his remark to Henry Corbin that Suzuki also did not repudiate Swedenborg and his teachings. In fact, in a memorial to Suzuki, Furuno Kiyoto wrote that he found Suzuki's basic thought to be more or less influenced by Swedenborg.[10] The Japanese Swedenborgian Nagashima Tatsuya has tentatively called Suzuki a "crypto-Swedenborgian," suggesting that his short-lived but intense engagement with Swedenborg's works determined his approach to religion in general.[11]

The question of influence is a tricky one, however. Suzuki and Swedenborg both produced such a huge volume of work that a determined investigator could probably locate any number of similarities. And although Suzuki was undoubtedly influenced by Swedenborg, he first viewed the Swedish mystic through a lens already shaped by Buddhism; Emerson's transcendentalism; German idealism; Monism; and, finally, the philosophy of William James. Sorting out the influences and affinities among these different strains of thought would be a long exercise in unraveling what largely comes down to a "chicken-and-egg" question.

In the end, Suzuki chose to use the term "Zen" to designate the universal truth that he perceived to be the foundation of all religion and philosophy. As early as 1895, when he was 25 years old, Suzuki wrote an essay revealingly entitled "The Zen of Emerson";[12] and years later, in *The Eastern Buddhist*, he explicitly stated:

> As I conceive it, Zen is the ultimate of all philosophy and religion. . . . Zen is not necessarily an offshoot of Buddhist philosophy alone. For I find it in Christianity, Mahommedanism, in Taoism, and even in Confucianism. . . . Zen is what makes the religious feeling run through its legitimate channel and what gives life to the intellect.[13]

It is clear that, despite his exposure to various schools of thought, Suzuki was most comfortable operating through the framework of Zen Buddhism. How then should we explain his interest in Swedenborg? Suzuki himself finds affinities between Swedenborgian thought and Buddhism in *Suedenborugu* and "Swedenborg's View of Heaven and 'Other-Power.'" But Suzuki's tendency to find the same truths in various religious systems and thinkers enabled him to draw from a host of sources throughout his career. To answer the question "Why, for a time, did Suzuki engage Swedenborg with such intensity?" and its corollary "Why did he later lose this intensity?" we should look not to timeless similarities, or "correspondences," that Suzuki may have found between Swedenborg and Buddhist thought, but instead to those unique qualities that made Swedenborg relevant for a particular period in his life. In short, an answer to these questions requires an explanation based not on theological resemblances, but on historical conditions.

On one level, Suzuki's interest in Swedenborg hinges on the simple fact that Swedenborg was "fashionable" in the late nineteenth and early twentieth centuries, claiming the attention of Henri Bergson, W.B. Yeats, William James, and many other prominent thinkers and writers.[14] Swedenborg was virtually unknown in Japan; but between 1897 and 1908, Suzuki lived in America, where Swedenborgian churches had proliferated throughout the nineteenth century. Encouraged by Zen Abbot Shaku Sôen, Suzuki spent eleven years in Illinois working for Paul Carus, a German immigrant who advocated the reconciliation of scientific and religious thinking through his "Religion of Science," or "Monism."[15] Immersed in the Monist project, Suzuki would have had ample exposure to Swedenborg, a man who accounted for his own mystical experiences and discoveries with the cool reason of a scientist.

But it was actually in London, on his way home to Japan in 1908, that Suzuki was invited to grapple in depth with a work by Swedenborg and translate it into Japanese. The London-based Swedenborg Society asked him to translate *Heaven and Hell*, which was then published in 1910. In that same year, Suzuki came back to England from Japan to serve as a "vice-president" at the International Swedenborg Congress.[16] He subsequently translated Swedenborg's *The New Jerusalem and Its Heavenly Doctrine* (1914), *Divine Love and Wisdom* (1914), and *Divine Providence* (1915).

Primed by his experience with Monism, Suzuki was willing to do the initial translation of *Heaven and Hell*, but how do we explain his continued interest in Swedenborg? The preface to *Suedenborugu* possesses an urgency that shows Suzuki had more than a casual interest in this Swedish mystic:

> Now, in Japan, the field of religious thought is finally reaching a state of crisis. Those who wish to cultivate their spirit, those who bemoan the times, must absolutely know of this person [Swedenborg]. This is the reason for this book.[17]

In the introduction following his preface, Suzuki explains more clearly what he means by an impending "crisis":

> Looking in particular at the current state of spiritual life in Japan, it seems that people are tired of the superficiality of our materialistic, industrial culture, but do not know where to turn. Both the government and the people feel the necessity for religion, yet it has not been adequately investigated how this need can be met.[18]

During his time in America, Japan had undergone rapid urbanization and industrialization. Strikes had increased in tandem with the number of factory workers, and more broad-based protests, like demonstrations in 1906 against a rise in streetcar fares, had become increasingly familiar. Educational policies had swelled the ranks of the managerial classes, who, though better off than manual laborers, also strained under the pressure of a modern, capitalist economy. Alienated by the demands of mechanized life, many in the educated middle class turned to a search for their "deepest selves."

This "move inward," as Thomas Rimer calls it, was especially pronounced among the youth of Japan's higher schools and universities.[19] After the Meiji restoration of 1868, the government orchestrated a massive effort to build modern institutions, including a national school system.[20] But by the turn of the century, Japan's privileged teenagers took these achievements for granted and spent more and more time in a search for personal meaning. This quest was shaped in large part by German idealism, proselytized by such figures as Raphael Koeber, professor of philosophy at Tokyo University from 1893 to 1914. "My students are all philosophers, and as philosophers they are soldiers fighting with spiritual arms for the expansion of the *Zeitgeist*," Koeber once said. Teacher-philosophers like Nishida Kitarô (who, incidentally, met Suzuki at age seventeen and was a lifelong friend) brought this zeal to the high-school level, forming extracurricular groups like the Goethe Reading Society.[21]

But others among Japan's elite regarded this exploration of the inner self to be unhealthy, for it undermined the Meiji ideal of the publicly engaged "gentleman" (*shinshi*), now needed more than ever to fortify the state against waves of social unrest. Anxiety about so-called "retreatism" (*taihoshugi*) was fueled by the 1903 suicide of Fujimura Misao, a highschool boy who leapt from the top of a three-hundred-foot cliff into the basin of Japan's spectacular Kegon waterfall. Before killing himself, he carved his epitaph, "Feelings at the Precipice," into an oak tree. His last words read, in part:

> There is, after all, only one word for truth: "incomprehensible."
> My agony over this question has brought me, at last, to a decision to die,
> And yet now, standing at the precipice,
> There is no anxiety in my heart.
> For the first time, I realize that great sorrow is at one with great happiness.[22]

Fujimura became a national celebrity, dying as he did not for family, school, or country, but for a purely "egocentric" cause.

Alarm over the loss of "state ideals," the symptoms of this loss being "retreatism" on the one hand and socialism on the other, increased through the first decade of the twentieth century and resulted in the *Boshin* Imperial Rescript of 1908. This document condemned the excesses of "private activity" and emphasized the importance of "uniting sentiments of high and low" through "national morality" (*kokumin dôtoku*).[23] The task of renovating civic virtue was embraced by Buddhist and Christian organizations alike, as well as by Shinto shrines, which were then being merged and abolished by the thousands to fulfill a government policy of administrative standardization.[24]

The government's force-fed morality only intensified the search among intellectuals for a preserve beyond the power of the state, a realm that increasingly went under the rubric of *bunka*, a Japanese approximation of the European word "culture."[25] This sacred space of personal cultivation, which transcended the secular world of politics and "machine civilization," was also frequently conflated with the realm of "religion" and "spirituality." In 1909, at the high school where Fujimura had committed suicide six years before, Debate Club members issued the following statement:

> Today the Debate Club is moving quickly in the direction of religious and spiritual matters. . . . Our attention to problems of the external world is diminishing, and there is a feeling that we should remove ourselves from direct involvement in dormitory politics.[26]

Replace the word "dormitory" with "state," and the above declaration sums up the attitude of many intellectuals in the wider society. Turning away from external affairs, such writers as Abe Jirô and Kurata Hyakuzô produced an angst-ridden, confessional literature that was popular among Japan's rapidly growing middle classes.

The producers of this literature rallied under the banner of "individualism" (*kojinshugi*). Yet they were criticized by reformists who appropriated the very same slogan. These included feminists, socialists, and other socially engaged individualists who were not only disdainful of public morality but out to change it.[27] Instead of viewing culture (or personalized "religion") as a cloister for permanent retreat, they saw it as a base from which to launch reformist social movements. Ikuta Chôkô, publisher of the magazine *Hankyô*, summed up this dialectical position when he wrote in 1914, "It is only by improving oneself that society can be improved; and it is only by improving society that one can improve himself."[28]

Suzuki also advocated an engaged individualism that was opposed to mindless statism on the one hand and self-centered introspection on the other. From 1909 to 1921, Suzuki taught English at the elite secondary school Gakushûin (Peer's School). While there, he warned his privileged students:

> Individualism is not selfishness; it means to become one's own master. From the standpoint of ethics, this is something lacking in young people today. Of course, individualism has dangers as well, but one should not disregard its merits. As for me, I will cling to its merits.[29]

Suzuki did not publicly advocate an egalitarian individualism. Echoing the *noblesse oblige* ethic of American liberalism, he instead exhorted the educated elite to take advantage of its privilege to help society.[30] Nevertheless, such sentiments were at odds with the martial spirit of Gen. Nogi Maresuke, head of the Gakushûin, who displayed his ethic of unquestioning loyalty when he followed the Meiji emperor into death in 1912. News of Nogi's suicide shocked the nation and whipped up a storm of debate. Some condemned the gesture as perverse and retrograde, while others praised its purity of spirit. Concerning his superior's action, Suzuki argued that it was not up to

others to judge Nogi but added that "those who imitate him
are fools."[31]

Upon the death of Emperor Meiji, and the devoted Gen. Nogi, Japan entered a new reign under the Emperor Taishô. The nation had already undergone wrenching changes in the years before, but the emperor's death seemed to many to punctuate the death of an old age and the birth of a new one. Worries that had led to the *Boshin* rescript of 1908 only intensified with the shift into Taishô. Defenders of the state and civic virtue were especially anxious about the new generation, which was, in the words of journalist Tokutomi Soho,

> all divided between disinterested, colorless youth and despairing youth who worry about the problems of life, success-oriented youth carried off by the fever of rising in the world [*risshin shusse*], and examples of youth without ambition. These are the youth of Taishô.[32]

The state's answer to these concerns was the promotion of "national morality" through its system of Shinto shrines and the Buddhist and Christian establishment. But amid this general sense of spiritual crisis, Suzuki prescribes a very different solution in his introduction to *Suedenborugu*. After noting the need for a renewed spirituality to counter the "superficiality of our materialistic, industrial culture," Suzuki writes:

> Of course, institutional religion is linked up to the nation as a whole; but in one respect, religion is thoroughly personal, governed by such things as the temperament, taste, education, and circumstances of the individual. Therefore, even the state is powerless to enforce religious devotion against people's will. Furthermore, people's hearts cannot be won merely through the inertia of tradition. Surely, religion bears fruit only from within, blooming naturally like a flower. So in response to the religious thirst in people's hearts, it is necessary to introduce various creeds and philosophies from many places and have

people choose according to what speaks to their individual tendencies.[33]

In opposition to the state's policy of standardization, Suzuki promotes a "free-market" of religious ideas. Instead of fighting the consumer ethic of modern Japan, he says, educators should accommodate it by stocking the spiritual supermarket with as many brands of thought as possible. Suzuki reiterates his opposition to state control of religion when he notes in the chapter on Swedenborg's "Character and Lifestyle" that Swedenborg was forced to publish his religious works in England and Holland because his homeland, Sweden, would not allow the spread of his unorthodox teachings.[34]

Suzuki could have chosen from a number of freethinkers to make his point, but it is Swedenborg's life that he decides to present as "a model for the individual." What makes Swedenborg so appealing? Although Suzuki certainly admires his theology, he is especially interested in portraying Swedenborg the *person*: "He was a man of spirit; and now, in the twentieth century, we are moved by the force of his personality. *If only for this reason, we should know about his life.*"[35]

In *Suedenborugu*, Suzuki divides this life into two halves, devoting a chapter to each. In chapter 1, Suzuki recounts Swedenborg's scientific accomplishments, pointing out that these were not limited to theoretical scholarship, but extended to such practical technologies as metallurgy and engineering. Swedenborg applied this knowledge while serving as "assessor extraordinary for the Bureau of Mines," a critical post in Sweden at the time. Suzuki mentions that Swedenborg also wrote a valuable work on fluctuations in the Swedish currency and published the first algebra text in Swedish. In order to accomplish these tasks, Swedenborg studied abroad in countries like Germany and Holland, where mathematics, physics, and other sciences of the European Enlightenment were more advanced.

The portrait we get of Swedenborg is of a practical young man intent on transmitting the knowledge of continental Europe to his homeland, and no Japanese reading this in 1913 would miss the parallel being drawn between Swedenborg in the early eighteenth century and the creators of the Meiji state in the mid- to late-nineteenth century. The "Meiji oligarchs" also went on missions to Europe to gain first-hand knowledge of modern institutions and introduce them to Japan, creating, as in Sweden's case, a nation-state that could compete with the rest of the modernized world. Swedenborg was a true *shinshi*, a gentleman of solid character who embodied the Meiji values of self-sacrifice and nationalism. He not only brought technical knowledge to his country, but also served in the House of Peers from the time his family was ennobled in 1719 (when Swedenborg was 31 years old). The fact that Swedenborg was not a commoner but a baron must have had particular salience for Suzuki, who was then teaching a mixture of English and liberal ethics to the sons of Japan's aristocracy.

In chapter 2, Suzuki recounts the mystical experiences that transformed Swedenborg's life, noting that these experiences at first caused him a great deal of anguish. But Swedenborg eventually accepted his revelations and poured the energy originally devoted to science into relating and interpreting his encounters with the spiritual world. This latter half of Swedenborg's life, in which he turned from his study of the external world to an exploration of the internal world, corresponds to the general "move inward" among intellectuals of late Meiji and Taishô Japan.

But Suzuki emphasizes that Swedenborg's turn to mysticism and religion did not constitute a complete rejection of his former self. He shows that Swedenborg brought the same kind of investigative enthusiasm to the spiritual world as he did to the physical world:

Feeling that his previous philosophical and scientific studies had been removed from the divine will and unrelated to his true calling, his attitude completely changed. However, from what I have seen, there is not a huge, unbreachable gap between Swedenborg's so-called worldly career and his spiritual career, since his earlier thoughts and sentiments show a continuity with his spiritual life. . . .[36]

After discussing the *Arcana Coelestia*, a multivolume exposition of the spiritual sense of the books of Genesis and Exodus, Suzuki also says:

One thing that should be noted here is that, despite producing such a great work, Swedenborg continued to fulfill his duties as a member of the House of Peers by voicing, *without any hesitation*, his commanding views on Sweden's public finances and administration. These opinions were not the vague, fanciful, and abstract statements commonly made by scholars and religious thinkers. His concrete plans always cut to the heart of the evils of his day.[37]

Here Suzuki criticizes angst-ridden individualists and their retreat from politics. He demonstrates that there does not have to be an "unbreachable gap" between the public duty of Meiji and the private introspection of Taishô. One can indeed try to improve society while pursuing personal enlightenment, and without caving in to state ideology. The realm of "culture" or "spirituality" should not be a permanent retreat from the world, but a place to learn how to overcome the bonds of the ego and help others instead. Suzuki stresses this point when he says that according to Swedenborg,

By faith alone salvation is impossible; we must acknowledge that not until charity and love are added is the fruit of salvation born. . . . From the start, it is crucial to have a penitent heart and, recognizing one's sins, to accumulate good deeds as befit love and wisdom.[38]

In his introduction, Suzuki also cites a defense of Swedenborg's religion by Count Anders von Höpken, who wrote that "This religion, in preference to, and in a higher degree than, any other, must produce the most honest and industrious subjects; for this religion properly places the worship of God in *uses*."[39] Later in the book, Suzuki further writes that Swedenborg's lifestyle was extremely simple and that he continued to be frugal and industrious until the day he died.

This promotion of religion as a means to build ethical character accords with a 1911 lecture that Suzuki gave on Zen Buddhism, which he portrayed at the time as a "moral anvil on which your character is hammered and hammered."[40] But, by the time he gave his 1936 lectures on Zen and Japanese culture in England and America (sponsored by the Japanese Foreign Ministry), Suzuki had stopped expressing such sentiments. In the face of increasing militarism and nationalism, he too retreated into a personalistic aesthetic. For example, contrast the previous statement on Zen as "moral anvil" with this claim from *Zen and Its Influence on Japanese Culture*, a book based mainly on his 1936 lectures:

> Art impulses are more primitive or more innate than those of morality. The appeal of art goes more directly into human nature. Morality is regulative, art is creative. One is an imposition from without, the other is an irrepressible expression from within. Zen finds its inevitable association with art but not with morality. Zen may remain unmoral but not without art. . . .[41]

Later in this same work Suzuki writes that Zen has no special doctrine or philosophy, so that "it may be found wedded to anarchism or fascism, communism or democracy, atheism or idealism, or any political or economic dogmatism."[42]

Suzuki thus painted himself into exactly the apolitical, culturalist corner that he had criticized through his work on Swedenborg years before. As Robert Sharf notes in "Zen and Japanese Nationalism,"[43] Suzuki also became increasingly chauvinistic. I am inclined not to condemn Suzuki for his cultural biases, because national pride is a powerful force to which even the most critical thinkers succumb. Furthermore, Kirita Kiyohide has pointed out that, unlike a host of other Zen Buddhists, Suzuki did not wholeheartedly support the military, but instead spent the 1930s and 1940s focusing on Buddhist scholarship.[44] Yet it is clear that Suzuki "did not take a firm stance against the war or write essays criticizing the military or Shinto nationalists head-on."[45] Not seeing any alternative, he retreated into a highly personalized religious aesthetic.

This shift away from sociohistorical concerns can already be detected in Suzuki's second (and last) work devoted exclusively to Swedenborg, "*Suedenborugu: Sono Tenkai to Tarikikan*" (Swedenborg's View of Heaven and 'Other-Power'), which was first written as an article in 1924 and then republished as a short chapter in his 1927 work *Zen: Miscellaneous Essays*. In the 1913 *Suedenborugu*, Suzuki made some comparisons between Swedenborgian and Buddhist thought, but these were overshadowed by his presentation of Swedenborg as an exemplary person. The later essay, in contrast, dispenses with Swedenborg's biography (aside from a bare-bones sketch in the last paragraph), and instead focuses on associating Swedenborg's heaven with the paradise of Pure Land Buddhism.[46]

As in so many of his writings, Suzuki is basically concerned here with resolving the apparent contradiction between free will and universal salvation, concepts spatially translated into our conditioned world on the one hand and paradise on the other. For example, earlier chapters in the 1927 book include "Self-Power and Other-Power," "Zen and Nenbutsu," and "Koan Zen and Nenbutsu Zen."[47] In all three of these essays, Suzuki tries to resolve the dissonance between the self-effort of Zen and the absolute faith of Pure Land teachings. To put his thinking in a nutshell, he concludes that Zen and Pure Land Buddhism both aim for the same goal of selflessness and that the decision to rely on other-power actually entails a measure of self-power, while self-power taken to an extreme eventually leads to an abandonment of the self and culminates in a reliance on other-power.

In the essay on Swedenborg, Suzuki again explores this issue through the Swedenborgian vocabulary of angels, innocence, divine love, and so on. Here he is not interested in portraying Swedenborg as an historical individual, but as a timeless mystic whose perception of truth differs from that of Buddhism in form, but not substance. After writing that the doctrine of correspondence can be fruitfully applied to Buddhist teachings, he speculates, "If Swedenborg had not communicated with the Christian heaven, and had instead mastered Buddhist philosophy, what kind of 'hidden will' would he have discovered?"[48] Ironically, because Suzuki found such a strong affinity between Buddhism and Swedenborgianism, Swedenborg largely disappeared from his later writings. Suzuki did make occasional references to the Swedish mystic; but, sufficiently stocked with Buddhist terminology, he had no more need for Swedenborg's particular imagery and doctrines. In time, Swedenborg became a "Buddha of the North," a figure in complete concordance with Suzuki's vision of Buddhism, yet missing the unique contingencies that gave the *Suedenborugu* of 1913 its special urgency. As Suzuki withdrew from the historical arena of social change, his interest in Swedenborg shifted from his earthly life to his eternal truths; and the latter, as he saw them, could just as well be expressed through the language of Buddhism, or, in a Christian context, through the works of someone like Meister Eckhart. Swedenborg, meanwhile, vanished into the thin air of Buddhahood.

Notes

1. This story is recounted in a footnote appearing in Corbin's *Creative Imagination in the Sufism of Ibn'Arabi*, trans. Ralph Manheim (Princeton: Princeton University Press, 1969) 354–355. The italics are Corbin's.

2. D.T. Suzuki, "Infinite Light," *Collected Writings on Shin Buddhism*, ed. Eastern Buddhist Society (Kyoto, Japan: Shinshû Ōtaniha, 1973), 152. An editor's note on page 129 reads, "This paper seems to have been written around 1950, most likely as a series of talks Dr. Suzuki gave in California which were later combined and rewritten to form this single essay."

3. According to this doctrine, all things in the physical, mundane world correspond to states in the spiritual world, which proceed in stages to their source in the Divine. Michael Stanley, a longtime student of Swedenborg's theology, compares this succession to a Chinese box, a "series of forms within forms, with the one Source [the Divine] at the centre of each and every form. . . . Higher forms give being and purpose to lower forms, which themselves can look to the higher forms on which they depend and which they serve." See Michael Stanley, *Emanuel Swedenborg: Essential Readings* (Wellingborough, UK: Aquarian Press, 1988), 20.

4. Daisetsu Teitarô Suzuki, "Zen to Tetsugaku," *Suzuki Daisetsu Zenshû*, ed. Hisamatsu Shin'ichi, Yamaguchi Susumu, and Furuta Shôkin, 30 volumes (Tokyo: Iwanami Shôten, 1968–1970), vol. 27, 41. In subsequent notes, Suzuki's collected works will be abbreviated *SDZ*.

5. D.T. Suzuki, *Mysticism: Christian and Buddhist*, ed. Ruth Nanda Anshen (New York: Harper & Bros., 1957), 116.

6. The references to Swedenborg listed here are not exhaustive.

There may be citations appearing elsewhere in the *SDZ*; furthermore, many of Suzuki's works have not been included in the *SDZ*. (A more comprehensive bibliography of Suzuki's Japanese works has been compiled by Kirita Kiyohide of Hanazono University, Kyoto, while an English list has been drawn up by Wayne Yokoyama of Ōtani University, Kyoto). Still, it is unlikely that any substantial work on Swedenborg would have gone undetected by scholars.

7. The present translation is based on the Japanese as it appears in *SDZ*, vol. 24, 3–67.

8. This essay (in Japanese, *"Suedenborugu: Sono Tenkai to Tarikikan"*) appears in *SDZ*, vol. 19, 634–642, as the last chapter in the book *Zen: Miscellaneous Essays* (in Japanese, *Zen: Zuihitsu*). This book was first published in 1927, but the chapter on Swedenborg was originally published in February 1924 in the journal *Chūgai Nippō*.

9. *SDZ*, vol. 19, 642.

10. Furuno Kiyoto, *"Suzuki Daisetsushi no Profairu"* (Profile of Suzuki Daisetsu), *Suzuki Daisetsu Zenshū Geppō* (*SDZ* newsletter), vol. 7, 1. The *Geppō* appear at the front of each volume of the *SDZ*.

11. Nagashima Tatsuya, "Daisetsu T. Suzuki, Internationally Known Buddhist: Crypto-Swedenborgian?" *New Church Life* (May 1993), 216-217.

12. Kirita Kiyohide, *"Seinen Suzuki Teitarō Daisetsu no Shakaikan"* ("Young D.T. Suzuki's Views on Society"), *Zengaku Kenkyū* 72 (Jan. 10, 1994): 21.

13. Suzuki, "Some Aspects of Zen Buddhism," *The Eastern Buddhist* 1, no. 5 (May 1922): 341–342.

14. Furuno also makes this point about the popularity of Swedenborg. See Furuno, 1.

15. Robert H. Sharf, "The Zen of Japanese Nationalism," *History of Religions* 33 (Aug. 1993): 13–16.

16. *Transactions of the International Swedenborg Congress, Held in Connection with the Celebration of the Swedenborg Society's Centenary, London College, July 4-8, 1910*, 2d ed. London: The Swedenborg Society, 1911. A photo of Suzuki, with the title of "vice-president" underneath, faces p. 352 of the *Transactions*. A

full-length view of this photograph is reproduced as the frontispiece of the present volume.

17. *SDZ*, vol. 24, 3.

18. Ibid., 11.

19. Thomas Rimer, ed., *Culture and Identity: Japanese Intellectuals during the Interwar Years* (Princeton: Princeton University Press, 1990).

20. In 1868, a group of rebel samurai completed the overthrow of the Tokugawa Shogunate (1600–1868) and installed the Meiji Emperor, who reigned until his death in 1912.

21. Donald Roden, *Schooldays in Imperial Japan* (Berkeley, CA: University of California Press, 1980), 160-161.

22. Ibid., 166.

23. Carol Gluck, *Japan's Modern Myths: Ideology in the Late Meiji Period* (Princeton: Princeton University Press, 1985), 271.

24. Pursued vigorously after the end of the Russo-Japanese War in 1905, the policy of *isson issha* (one village, one shrine) translated into the merger and abolition of tens of thousands of shrines. This strategy to reorient people's affiliations and practices caused great anxiety and was implemented despite protest from those priests and parishioners whose traditional independence was at stake. But by the time Suzuki wrote *Suedenborugu* in 1913, the state's redistribution of Shinto shrines was a *fait accompli*. See Helen Hardacre, *Shintô and the State: 1868-1988* (Princeton: Princeton University Press, 1989), 38; 98.

25. H.D. Harootunian, "Introduction: A Sense of an Ending and the Problem of Taishô," in *Japan in Crisis: Essays On Taishô Democracy*, ed. Bernard S. Silberman and H. D. Harootunian (Princeton: Princeton University Press, 1974), 15–18.

26. Roden, 211.

27. For an in-depth discussion of the varieties of individualism at this time, see Sharon Hamilton Nolte, "Individualism in Taishô Japan," *Journal of Asian Studies* (Aug. 1984): 667–684.

28. Matsuo Takayoshi, "A Note on the Political Thought of Natsume Sôseki in His Later Years," *Japan in Crisis*, 69.

29. Kirita Kiyohide, "D.T. Suzuki on Society and the State," in *Rude Awakenings: Zen, the Kyoto School, and the Question of Na-*

tionalism, ed. James Heisig and John C. Maraldo (Honolulu, HI: University of Hawaii Press, 1995), 57–58.

30. "Most of you are children of the nobility. You form a special class in Japan and receive privileged treatment from the imperial family. You must remember that wherever special favor is shown, special responsibility is also demanded. . . . Natural ability means not claiming for your own that which does not belong to you and not entrusting yourself to good fortune. It is, in a sense, individualism. The only way to develop your natural abilities is to make full use of your independence and freedom. . . ." Ibid., 57.

31. Ibid.

32. Harootunian, 10.

33. *SDZ*, vol. 24, 11.

34. *SDZ*, vol. 24, 50.

35. *SDZ*, vol. 24, 8. Italics are mine.

36. *SDZ*, vol. 24, 21.

37. *SDZ*, vol. 24, 28. Italics are mine.

38. *SDZ*, vol. 24, 38.

39. *SDZ*, vol. 24, 11–12. Italics are mine.

40. D.T. Suzuki, *Essays in Zen Buddhism: First Series* (New York: Grove Weidenfeld, 1949), 29. This passage appears in the introduction to the *Essays*, which were first published in 1927. A footnote says that this introduction was originally written as "one of the popular lectures prepared by the author for students of Buddhism, 1911."

41. D.T. Suzuki, *Zen Buddhism and Its Influence on Japanese Culture* (Kyoto, Japan: The Eastern Buddhist Society, 1938), 21.

42. Ibid., 36.

43. Sharf, 25-29.

44. Kirita, "D.T. Suzuki on Society and the State," 60–61.

45. Ibid., 62. Differing perspectives on the relationship between nationalism and Zen Buddhist thinkers like Suzuki are presented in *Rude Awakenings.*

46. Adherents of Pure Land Buddhism aim for salvation in Amida Buddha's Pure Land, a paradise where all sentient beings can attain enlightenment. While he was still a *bodhisattva*, or a being on the path to buddhahood, Amida made the following vow: "If, after

I have attained buddhahood, sentient beings in the ten directions who have sincere minds, serene faith, and a desire to be born in my country, should not be born there even with ten *nenbutsu* recitations [*Namu Amida Butsu*, 'Homage to Amida Buddha'], may I not attain perfect enlightenment. . . ." From Hisao Inagaki, *A Dictionary of Japanese Buddhist Terms* (Union City, CA: Heian International, 1989), 109.

47. In Japanese, *"Jiriki to Tariki," "Zen to Nenbutsu,"* and *"Koan Zen to Nenbutsu Zen." Jiriki* denotes the ability to save oneself, while *tariki,* in contrast, refers to the saving power of a Buddha or *bodhisattva*. Zen meditation is typically associated with the former, and the Pure Land practice of calling Amida Buddha's name *(nenbutsu)* with the latter. A *koan* is a question, dialogue, or story, frequently paradoxical, that is used by Zen practitioners as an object of meditation.

48. *SDZ*, vol 19, 524.

PART ONE

Swedenborg

A Translation of Suedenborugu

D. T. Suzuki, 1958

Preface to Suedenborugu

Revolutionary in theology, traveler of heaven and hell, champion of the spiritual world, king of the mystical realm, clairvoyant unique in history, scholar of incomparable vigor, scientist of penetrating intellect, gentleman free of worldly taint: all of these combined into one make Swedenborg. Now, in Japan, the field of religious thought is finally reaching a state of crisis. Those who wish to cultivate their spirit, those who bemoan the times, must absolutely know of this person. This is the reason for this book.

October 1913[1]

CHAPTER I

Introduction

Swedenborg's name is relatively unknown to people in Japan. When we speak of Martin Luther, John Wesley, George Fox, and John Calvin, those who are somewhat interested in Western religion probably know their names. However, very few people know that about 150 years ago there was a Swedish theologian unique in history. Not only did he make personal tours of heaven and hell, but he also had audiences with important personages in heaven and, consulting with them, made new discoveries in theology, philosophy, and psychology.

Even among those who have heard his name, there are probably very few who believe that he is relevant to today's culture and thought. If such people exist, they consider him to be an extraordinary psychological phenomenon and make him into a mere piece of data for research. However, those who study Emanuel Swedenborg in earnest discover that he is a very interesting subject for investigation from a number of angles.

First of all, Swedenborg said that he traveled in heaven and hell and witnessed in detail the actual state of people after death. His statements are quite sincere. They are free of the slightest exaggeration and, viewed from the standpoint of common sense, seem to accord well with the truth. This is the first reason that Swedenborg is of interest.

In this world of ours, there seems to be a spiritual realm separate from that of the five senses; and when we enter a certain psychological state, we apparently can communicate with that realm. Even if we think that the circumstances of this other realm have no moral connection whatsoever to the mundane world, there is plenty that is of interest to science and philosophy. This is a second reason to examine Swedenborg.

Swedenborg's theological doctrines greatly resemble those of Buddhism. He taught that, having discarded the *proprium*,[2] one must act in accordance with the workings of the Divine, that true salvation is the harmonious unification of belief and action, and that the Divine manifests itself as wisdom and love. Furthermore, he says that love is greater and more profound than wisdom and that there is nothing great or small that is beyond the reach of divine providence. There is not a single thing in the world left to chance, and one can witness the revelation of divine wisdom and divine love even in the stroke of a pen, for it is deeply imbued with divine providence. These sorts of issues attract the interest of religious scholars, and especially Buddhists. This is the third reason that we should study Swedenborg.

Just one of the above three points makes Swedenborg a man worth studying. He also is historically unique. When we consider how difficult it is to find a similar example, we cannot help but feel that he must not be neglected. The fact that scientific and religious genius marvelously combined to produce a person of such unfathomable depth makes not only good material from the viewpoint of psychological research; but because he was a man of great vitality and distinction who had escaped the taint of worldliness, his life also serves as a model for the individual, teaching numerous lessons. There are no drastic changes in the course of his biography, so there is nothing that especially dazzles us. But his eighty-four years of life were completely devoted to science and religion, his everyday existence filled with infinite wonders. He was a man of spirit; and now, in the twentieth century, we are moved by the force of his personality. If only for this reason, we should know about his life.

When we read his works, investigate his biography, and look into his thought, we feel as if Swedenborg's person appears before our eyes. He is a likable old man, with an aura of renunciation flowing from his brow. Even though his physical body cannot be disentangled from the troubles of this defiled world, his mind's eye is always filled with the mysteries of heaven. As he walks through the mist, a wonderful joy seems to well up and play beneath his feet. If someone asks the old man about such things as the way of heaven, like a mountain stream that is never exhausted, he patiently and repeatedly expounds it. His accounts do not resemble bizarre illusions at all. He relates them no differently than if they were mundane events in our world of the five senses. Listeners are shocked, their minds probably bewildered. Nevertheless, he coolly regards these things as if they were daily fare. This is why it is not easy to fathom him.

Given his character and teachings, Swedenborg ought to be known to the world at large. He should be circulated among us much like his contemporaries Kant and Wesley. However, there are two main reasons that only a handful of people believe his words.

One is that his writing is extremely verbose. He repeats the same things again and again, giving the impression of an old man teaching a child. Generally, whether or not your name is passed on to future generations does not depend on the loftiness of your ideas. There are many cases of people's ideas being passed on, even if they are mediocre, due to their skillful rhetoric. It is common for people to be inclined to listen to someone who is dignified and charismatic, even if what he says is not particularly clever. The foremost wish of the masses is always to have their senses gratified. So, as they say, the loftier the melody, the fewer the people in harmony. The teachings of Mencius may not be as logically constructed as those of Hsün Tzu, but people are more often pleased by Mencius because his writing is elegant, while Hsün Tzu's is plain and unspectacular. However, Hsün Tzu's way of reasoning surpasses that of Mencius. Viewed only from the standpoint of his logic, Hsün Tzu should be widely read.[3] Swedenborg's case is also like this. If his prose were elegant and eye-catching, he would be loudly acclaimed by the public.

Secondly, because his statements concern a world that is separate from our world of the senses, ordinary people find many of them difficult to believe. This is compounded by the fact that he speaks of these sorts of things without so much as lifting an eyebrow, as if they were common fare. He is very matter-of-fact and does not speak extravagantly, something that makes readers suspicious. They might doubt whether the author really had such an experience and ask how it is that the things he says depart so much from common sense. Judging from how calmly he speaks about these things, they might consider him insane and wonder whether they can believe in the words of a madman.

A third reason is that people think his descriptions too specific. If they are beyond ordinary understanding, then to enter into such detail, to explain circumstances in full, gives rise to doubt. It seems that people like Ralph Waldo Emerson could not completely devote themselves to Swedenborg because of this fact. For instance, if Swedenborg had only said that there is a hell and a heaven, many people would probably believe him. But he contends that such-and-such a person is currently in anguish in the scorching heat of hell and that certain famous historical figures exist in the first level of heaven. Speaking personally with these people and listening to them, he discovered that their opinions had changed greatly since they had left our world. When he claims such things, readers are shocked, because the descriptions seem all too real. I believe that one reason people in this world have not been receptive to Swedenborg is that they think that he relates things in too much detail.

In the final analysis, however, such matters are insignificant. We should have faith in the whole and not call logical possibilities into doubt. Swedenborg's accounts are consistent and have an air of sincerity and honesty about them. He is by no means a deceptive person. He relates things only as he has seen and heard them, without any embellishments. Whether one believes him or not is another problem, but there is certainly a valid source for this kind of sincerity that is worth investigating. Considering that this fact is of special relevance to our moral and religious life, we must not ignore it.

Looking in particular at the current state of spiritual life in Japan, it seems that people are tired of the superficiality of our materialistic, industrial culture but do not know where to turn. Both the government and the people feel the necessity for religion, yet no one has adequately investigated how this need can be met. Of course, institutional religion is linked up to the nation as a whole; but in one respect, religion is thoroughly personal, governed by such things as the temperament, taste, education, and circumstances of the individual. Therefore, even the state is powerless to enforce religious devotion against people's will. Furthermore, people's hearts cannot be won merely through the inertia of tradition. Surely, religion bears fruit only from within, blooming naturally like a flower. So in response to the religious thirst in people's hearts, it is necessary to introduce various creeds and philosophies from many places and have people choose according to what speaks to their individual tendencies. Of course, one does not have to believe in all of Swedenborg's claims, but one also cannot say that there are not diamonds in the rough. Jewels, in whichever world, are jewels. It would be foolish to reject them simply because they come in a strange package.

I believe that studying Swedenborg in present-day Japan is extremely beneficial, and I will now give my reasons. Count Anders von Höpken, who was prime minister of Sweden during Swedenborg's lifetime, and knew him for forty-two years, once sent a letter to a friend, saying:

> I have sometimes told the King that, if ever a new colony were to be formed, no religion could be better, as the prevailing and established one, than that developed by Swedenborg from the Sacred Scriptures, and this for the two following reasons: (1) This religion, in preference to, and in a higher degree than, any other, must produce the most honest and industrious subjects; for this religion properly places the worship of God in uses. (2) It causes least fear of death, as this religion regards death as merely a transition from one state to another, from a worse to a better situation; nay, upon his principles, I look upon death as being of hardly greater moment than drinking a glass of water.[4]

The truth of what Count von Höpken once said is not lost on anyone today.

During the summer of 1910,[5] an international conference was held in London to commemorate the founding of the Swedenborg Society one hundred years before. I would like to share here a portion of the inaugural address, which was given at the opening of the conference by the elected president, Dr. Edward John Broadfield. The speech was a very evenhanded account of Swedenborg's character, achievements, and studies:

> We are here honouring Swedenborg, probably from different points of view. There are some who regard him as an illustri-

ous and far-seeing man of science; others who honour him as a luminous and original philosopher; and a still larger number who look to him as an enlightened seer and a Heaven-directed theologian. But we all agree that he was a many-sided man, one of the profoundest students of his century, and, to adopt the words of Frederick Denison Maurice, we all recognize him as one of the great geniuses of his age. But whether you look at Swedenborg as a poet, as a philosopher, as a man of science, or as a theologian, you find in his career and in the successive ranges of his studies and investigations a remarkable series of well-defined gradations. He advanced from stage to stage, but every stage was preparatory to its successor; and those of us who consider his Illumination as the starting-point of his greatest period, recognize in all his previous experience an all-embracing time of preparation. In thinking of him merely as a subject of biography, one is reminded of a great mountain rising from the plain, stately and symmetrical when seen from a distance, on which, as we approach nearer, we see peak rising above peak, and so much grandeur hitherto unsuspected that we find it difficult to make anything like a general survey. Something like this, I think, all who ever made a systematic study of the life and works of Swedenborg must have felt. And the more closely we follow the incidents of his career, the more confidently may we say that during his eighty years he wore untarnished the white flower of a blameless life. He was unspoiled by fame. The favour of kings and princes never impaired his modesty, and the recognition of the splendour of his achievements never excited his vanity. He never claimed priority in discovery, though others have often, with perfect justification, done this for him; and this modesty was characteristic of him throughout life. From the first, too, in his studies in science and philosophy, he recognized the supreme power of an all-loving, Infinite Deity, and he never seemed to think that he had finished his inquiries unless he had discovered from them something to help his fellow creatures. He strove always, indeed, for the practical; and perhaps many here present will be surprised to hear of the extent of his powers of invention. The list of his discoveries, descriptions of which he always wrote down carefully, is almost unparalleled; and as a man of science his range of study extended from Mathematics and Physics to Astronomy, Mineralogy, Chemistry, Metallurgy, Anatomy, Physiology, Geology and Natural History. As a philosopher he studied all the systems known to his own time; and his own contributions to the study of different branches of philosophy were both far-reaching and original. Then he was a politician, an economist, a practical student of currency and finance, and in all these subjects he achieved distinction.[6]

CHAPTER 2

The First Half
of Swedenborg's Life

Emanuel Swedenborg was born in Stockholm, Sweden, on January 29, 1688, into a family that originally had farmed and later owned a number of mines. At the time, his father was an army chaplain. Afterwards, he advanced to become a dean and then a professor of theology at Uppsala University. Finally, he was made bishop of Skara. Emanuel was this man's second child. At that point he was called "Swedberg"; but in 1719, when Emanuel was 31 years old, Queen Ulrika Eleonora ennobled the household and gave it the name "Swedenborg." In this way, Emanuel was given a seat in the House of Peers and put in the position of helping to devise national policy. Not much about Swedenborg's childhood is known, only a letter that he wrote to a friend in his later years, which reads, in part:

> From my fourth to my tenth year my mind was constantly occupied with thoughts about God, salvation, and the spiritual affections of man. I often revealed things in my discourse which filled my parents with astonishment, and made them declare at times that certainly the angels spoke through my mouth. From my sixth to my twelfth year it was my greatest delight to converse with the clergy about faith; to whom I often observed that charity or love is the life of faith, and this vivifying charity or love is no other than the love of one's neighbor; that God vouchsafes this faith to every one, but that it is adopted only by such as practice that charity.[7]

Apparently, Swedenborg had a strong inclination from childhood toward religion. It goes without saying that he was influenced by his family's instruction; but in view of the fact that the maturity of his statements amazed his parents, he must have possessed religious genius. When he was eleven years old, he entered Uppsala University and chose to study linguistics, mathematics, mining, and natural philosophy. His thesis dealt with the Roman philosopher Seneca, as well as [Publilius Syrus] Mimus,[8] and he is said to have delivered his opinions on ethics with the robust force of a mature adult. At this time, he also translated the twelfth chapter of Ecclesiastes into Latin, which was published together with his father's writing.[9] The verses are poetically refined and reveal his mastery of the classics. His later works are written entirely in fluent and clear Latin: there is no instance where one might say his pen could not keep up with his ideas.

After Swedenborg left the university in 1710, he studied abroad for five years. He traveled to England, Holland, France, and Germany, learning a great deal. Lamenting the slow progress of mathematics and physics in his homeland, he proposed to Uppsala University that it was imperative to employ professors in advanced mathematics, even if that meant reducing its chairs in theology and history. To put mechanics into actual practice, he also mastered technologies alongside watchmakers, tools craftsmen, and lens grinders. Among his mechanical inventions were an airplane, a submarine, a machine gun, an air pump, and a self-playing piano. We can see, therefore, how modern he was. Around this time, he said in a letter, "I wish I had some more of these novelties, aye, a novelty in literary matters for every day in the year, so that the world might find pleasure in them. There are enough in one century who plod on in the old beaten track, while there are scarcely six or ten in a whole century, who are able to generate novelties which are based upon argument and reason."[10]

Swedenborg's spirit at the time certainly made the rest of the world pale in comparison.

His studies abroad were limited to the so-called physical sciences, consisting entirely of subjects like mathematics and physics. But even though it seems as if the religious and literary tendencies of his youth were eclipsed, he continued to write poetry in Latin, so his taste for literature had apparently not dried up and disappeared. Also, if we remember that the object of his research was gradually progressing toward ultimate truth, it is clear that his religious spirit attained increasingly mature stages.[11]

After returning home, Swedenborg published a journal devoted to mathematics, *Daedalus Hyperboreus* [The Northern Inventor], under the patronage of King Charles XII, although publication ceased two years later due to a lack of financing. In 1718 (when he was 31 years old), Swedenborg published a book on algebra, the first to be written in Swedish [*Regel-konsten författad i tijo böcker*]. Because mathematical studies were so far behind [in Sweden], he was understandably afraid that there was no one who could proofread the text.

Before traveling abroad, he had become acquainted with Christopher Polhem, the great engineer known at the time as "Sweden's Archimedes." After his return home, he was made Polhem's assistant by royal decree and appointed assessor extraordinary for the Bureau of Mines. Even though this post did not come with much of a salary, Swedenborg's genius and ability were recognized by the king.

Two years later, Charles XII attacked Norway, and Swedenborg transported ships a distance of seventeen miles overland for the king. His writing at this time concerned studies in mathematics and engineering, for example, "The Manufacture of Copper Sheets and Their Use," "Tide Levels of Ancient Times," and "Information on Docks, Canal Locks, and Salt Works."[12] During the time that Swedenborg, the young and able mathematician and engineer, served as Polhem's assistant and apprentice, he constantly traveled to and from Polhem's home. He eventually fell in love with Polhem's second oldest daughter, Emerentia. Although she was still a young girl of 14, both her father and the king were glad that she should become Swedenborg's future wife and gave their consent. However, when Emerentia grew older, she did not wish to be engaged to Swedenborg. He was in great despair and discouraged that she wanted to break off the engagement; but not wishing to make his loved one forever distressed because of him, he relinquished his claim on her. Throughout the rest of his life, he never thought again of marriage, but single-mindedly pursued his studies. As a result of this rebuff, he ended up gaining a lifetime free from encumbrances and came to think of nothing else but the divine will. It may be, then, that the divine will was at work from the start.

In 1721, at the age of 33, Swedenborg traveled abroad and published in Amsterdam a work on chemistry and physics [*Prodromus principiorum rerum naturalium, sive novorum tentaminum chymian et physicam experimentalem geometrice explicandi*]. This precursor to his later masterpiece *Principia* tried to reduce natural phenomena to a geometrical system. Beyond that, there were works on mineralogy and astronomy. Swedenborg went from Holland to Germany, and in 1723, in both Leipzig and Hamburg, published works on physics and mineralogy. Each of these works was the result of in-depth research in its field. Swedenborg's main purpose during these travels was to inspect the mines of different countries, gaining firsthand insights. All of his travel expenses were paid by Duke Ludwig Rudolph of Brunswick. After traveling for fifteen months, he returned to Sweden.

Upon returning home, Swedenborg immediately published a work on fluctuations in the Swedish currency. We do not currently know about the book's particulars; but judging from the fact that it was reprinted in Uppsala fifty years after it was first published, there must have been valuable material in it.[13] It seems that Swedenborg had an established reputation for his views on monetary debates.

Swedenborg began fulfilling his duties as assessor of the Bureau of Mines after his second trip abroad; and for the next eleven years, he did a great deal of research into both practical applications and scholarship. Throughout this period, Swedenborg's practice and learning increased in brilliance.

During this time, the chair in mathematics at the University of Uppsala was vacant, so Swedenborg was invited to fill it. But since his main interest was not in pure mathematics, he declined.

In 1733, in the spring of his 45th year, Swedenborg again traveled abroad and published *Principia* in Leipzig, the first volume of his great work *Opera Philosophica et Mineralia* [Philosophical and Mineralogical Works], which consists of three volumes. This so-called "philosophy" is not what we mean by the word *philosophy* today, but is instead the geometric observation of the structure of the universe. According to Swedenborg's explanation, there exists the infinite; and from the existence of this free and independent infinite all things are born. Within the infinite there is pure movement, which gives rise to a point. From this single point all things emerge. Broadly speaking, there is a force that creates movement within the single body of the infinite, and the endless variety created by this force is our universe. The form of this movement is always twisted in a spiral. Swedenborg applies this principle to the phenomenon of magnetism and then explains the process of the world's emergence, as well as the organization of the animal, plant, and mineral kingdoms. We see, then, that this masterpiece is the result of many years of research in the physical sciences. In the field of mineralogy, he made precise empirical and scientific observations about metals such as iron, copper, and brass, thus making a great contribution to the scientific world of his time. Swedenborg's scientific studies were recognized in his lifetime and by later generations.

In 1734, Swedenborg also published a small pamphlet entitled *Outlines of a Philosophical Argument on the Infinite*,[14] which can be regarded as a supplement to the *Principia*. Due to these works, Swedenborg is now famous throughout Europe; one after another, scholars from different countries look to his teachings.

For the two years between 1734 and 1736, Swedenborg stayed in his native land. During that period, he lost his father and acquired a fair inheritance. Outside of the salary he made as assessor, this inheritance would henceforth support his travels, writing, and independent lifestyle. In the summer of 1736, he again went abroad, this time to publish his new works. During his travels, he kept a diary, and it demonstrates a very broad scope of observations and interests. This great variety, all of which is treated with a keen critical eye, ranges from salt production and metallurgy to military drills. It also includes the pros and cons of each polity, the aesthetic and moral character of religious ceremonies, the charms of the opera, architecture, and works of art.

While abroad, Swedenborg stayed mainly in Germany, France, and Italy, where he seems to have finished both *The Economy of the Animal Kingdom* and his masterpiece *The Animal Kingdom*.[15] The general features of these books had appeared previously in some pamphlets, and drafts had been published over the course of several years; but Swedenborg's research during these travels allowed him to complete the fine points of the books. These two works were published in Holland and London. This was an advance from his previous research into the inorganic world, for his study of the organic world, and particularly the human body, was truly profound. His thirteen years of study, starting with the *Principia* and culminating in the publication of these works, had led Swedenborg to investigate the structure of the human body. From here he would advance further, not stopping until he had entered the spiritual world.

These two books were the last that Swedenborg would publish concerning worldly life. Even though some works remain in draft form, he had no desire to publish anything more; for soon after, he had his unprecedented encounter with the spiritual realm and underwent a complete transformation. Feeling that his previous philosophical and scientific studies had been removed from the divine will and unrelated to his true calling, his attitude completely changed. However, from what I have seen, there is not a huge, unbreachable gap between Swedenborg's so-called worldly career and his spiritual career, since his earlier thoughts and sentiments show a continuity with his spiritual life. Of course, there occurred a revolution in his writing, ideas, concepts, and arguments. Nevertheless, there were aspects of the past that remained in the background. To investigate the traces of this connection, we can look at what Swedenborg wrote in *The Animal Kingdom*, and see where his ideas were leading:

> I intend to examine, physically and philosophically, the whole Anatomy of the Body; of all its Viscera, Abdominal and Thoracic; of the Genital Members of both sexes; and of the Organs of the Five Senses. Likewise,
>
> The Anatomy of all parts of the Cerebrum, Cerebellum, Medulla Oblongata, and Medulla Spinalis.
>
> Afterwards, the cortical substance of the two brains; and the fibre;[16] and the causes of the forces and motion of the whole organism: Diseases, moreover; those of the head particularly, or which proceed by defluxion from the Cerebrum.

I purpose afterwards to give an introduction to Rational Psychology, consisting of certain new doctrines, through the assistance of which we may be conducted, from the material organism of the Body, to a knowledge of the Soul, which is immaterial: these are, the Doctrine of Forms; the Doctrine of Order and Degrees; also, the Doctrine of Series and Society; the Doctrine of Influx; the Doctrine of Correspondence and Representation: lastly, the Doctrine of Modification.

From these doctrines I come to the Rational Psychology itself; which will comprise the subjects of action; of external and internal sense; of imagination and memory; also, of the affections of the animus. Of the intellect, that is, of thought and of the will; and of the affections of the rational mind: also, of instinct.

Lastly, of the Soul; and of its state in the Body, its intercourse, affection, and immortality; and of its state when the body dies. The work to conclude with a Concordance of Systems.

From this summary or plan, the reader may see, that the end I propose to myself in the work, is a knowledge of the soul; since this knowledge will constitute the crown of my studies. . . . In order, therefore, to follow up the investigation, and to solve the difficulty, I have chosen to approach by the analytic way; and I think I am the first who has taken this course professedly. . . .

In olden time, before any racer could merit the crown, he was commanded to run seven times round the goal, which also I have determined here to do. . . .

Thus I hope, that by bending my course inwards continually, I shall open all the doors that lead to the soul, and enter directly within: by the divine permission.[17]

Thus we can see that there was not a complete division between the spiritual life of Swedenborg's later years and the intellectual life of his earlier years. In 1744, when he turned 56, he had an unprecedented spiritual experience and embarked

on a new life. It is not that this life had no connection to the
past. In one sense, it should be viewed as nothing more than
an extension of that previous life. Granted, his so-called "con-
templation of the Divine" may have differed from what he had
anticipated; but that is inconsequential from the perspective of
his entire life's development.

Swedenborg tried looking into the life of the Divine from intellectual and analytical angles. At first, he made a careful
study of chemistry, physics, and engineering; continuing from
there, he entered into biological and anatomical research. At
this point, using all of his theoretical genius, he tried to penetrate the mystery of the Divine, but he was not fully satisfied.
As a result of meditation and esoteric practice, his mind's eye
gradually grew clearer, and he apparently gained the won-
drous ability to enter and leave the realm of the Divine at will.
Swedenborg himself considered his experience a result of
God's grace; and his adherents similarly believe that, due to
this experience, Swedenborg was favored by God. But even
though [Swedenborg's proponents] think that no technology
or science can give rise to such an experience, I privately feel
that this is not necessarily so.

Swedenborg wrote one book during the transition from his
intellectual to his spiritual career. Called *The Worship and
Love of God*, it was published in London in 1745.[18] In this
book, he discarded the mathematical format of the earlier
Principia and discussed the creation of the universe in artistic
and physical terms. For Swedenborg, God was a wellspring of
the sciences, and he considered the traces of wisdom and inge-
nuity appearing in the universe to derive from the divine
power's foresight and salvation.[19] Swedenborg's thoughts and
sentiments clearly took on more and more of a religious color;
and when he underwent his transformation, he immediately
wished to activate the religious aspect of his character. Never,

in the spiritual life of his latter years, was anything accomplished by chance. Gradually, he grew in stages, as naturally as a tree sprouts buds, puts forth leaves, blooms with flowers, and bears fruit. Of course, the outcome of his growth differed greatly from what he had first expected, but it can still be considered a natural maturation.

Swedenborg's spiritual encounters seem to have begun in 1744, when he was 56. At that point, he was a genius who had excelled as a scientist. In regard to mining, mathematics, engineering, crystallography, astronomy, etc., he did not merely reiterate the theories of those who had preceded him. Even in such fields as anatomy, psychology, and philosophy, he advanced views that challenged those of his contemporaries, and he anticipated many theories of our own age. Today, eminent scholars in various fields recognize his contributions, and further comment on my part would be superfluous. But more importantly, it was in the latter part of his life that Swedenborg realized his true nature, establishing his special and enduring position in the religious world and providing unprecedented research topics for psychology. Entering into this life in one stroke, he dismissed his scientific ambitions and entirely gave up his previous intellectual plans. With all of his talent and spiritual strength, he devoted himself to his new career. Again, this is the main subject of this book. If it had not been for the life of his latter years, Swedenborg would have been admired in future generations only by eminent scientists. Heaven's will is always beyond people's ken, and nothing is settled until the coffin is shut.

CHAPTER 3

The Second Half
of Swedenborg's Life

Swedenborg's spiritual experiences did not begin suddenly but came gradually. It was not as if he were thrust one day into his new life. His encounters accumulated one after the other, finally giving rise to the determination to abandon his former intellectual life. Until then, he was, of course, filled with considerable anguish and struggle. At any rate, one of his first encounters occurred in 1745. He was in London, at the height of his mental engagement with various metaphysical works, when one evening, as always, he sat down to dinner. Taking now from what Swedenborg himself [purportedly] said:

> I was hungry, and ate with a good appetite. Towards the close of the meal I noticed a sort of dimness before my eyes . . . and I then saw the floor covered with the most horrid crawling reptiles, such as snakes, frogs, and similar creatures. . . . At last the darkness increased still more; but it disappeared all at once, and I then saw a man sitting in a corner of the room; as I was then alone, I was very much frightened at his words, for he said: "Eat not so much." All became black again before my eyes, but immediately it cleared away, and I found myself alone in the room.
>
> Such an unexpected terror hastened my return home; I did not let the landlord notice anything; but I considered well what had happened, and could not look upon it as a mere matter of chance, or as if it had been produced by a physical cause.

I went home; during the night, the same man revealed himself to me again, but I was not frightened now. He then said that he was the Lord God, the Creator of the world, and the Redeemer, and that He had chosen me to explain to men the spiritual sense of the Scripture, and that He Himself would explain to me what I should write on this subject; that same night also were opened to me, so that I became thoroughly convinced of their reality, the worlds of spirits, heaven, and hell, and I recognized there many acquaintances of every condition in life. From that day I gave up the study of all worldly science, and laboured in spiritual things, according as the Lord had commanded me to write. Afterwards the Lord daily opened my soul's eyes, so that in the middle of the day I could see into the other world, and in a state of perfect wakefulness converse with angels and spirits.[20]

Swedenborg related the above narrative to his friend Carl Robsahm. Judging from this [report], it seems that he was prepared to discard his intellectual life without any trouble. But then again, according to other records, after having these sorts of experiences, he would be distressed day and night for quite some time.

Swedenborg possessed scientific genius and learning to such a degree that he eclipsed the rest of his generation. After enjoying extraordinary success in the field of science, he continued to be burdened with the expectations of others. Then, suddenly, he discarded his achievements and did not look back. Not depending on his own efforts or intellect, he would become an instrument of God's revelation. Today we can only imagine how much turmoil and anguish was in Swedenborg's heart.

For example, it is similar to a Buddhist who believes in self-power turning around and becoming a believer in other-power. Belief in other-power seems easy, but its austerities are

no different from those entailed by relying on self-power.[21]
Those who spend their lives in religious practice know this
fact from personal experience. In April of 1744, during Easter
week, Swedenborg went to church.[22] While in line for communion, he heard the hymn "Jesus is my best of friends."[23]
Returning home afterwards, the bud of his heart opened, and
he perceived its green color. That night, he felt a peace of
boundless purity. Feeling just as if he had risen into heaven, he
cried out, "To the Highest be praise, honor and glory! . . .
Holy, holy, Lord God Zebaoth!"[24] He also said, "God's will
be done; I am Thine and not mine. God give His grace for this
[work]; for it is not mine."[25]

In this manner, Swedenborg leapt away in one bound from
his former scholarly concerns; and from this point until his
death, he spent all twenty-eight years realizing the word of
God. Swedenborg's spiritual activity in these twenty-eight years
was so impressive that it would have surprised him [if he had
known what was to come] when he was still in his prime of life.

Like other religious reformers, Swedenborg did not work on
a practical level but poured his efforts entirely into his writing.
In other words, seeing with his spiritual eye the structure, contents, and activities of heaven and hell and the conditions in
which the angels, spirits, and devils of these regions existed, he
worked assiduously to transmit to people as much as the divine will would allow. He believed without doubt that he was
a spiritual instrument for the fulfillment of God's commands,
so he was diligent in his work and did not weary of his labors
in the slightest. After receiving his mission, he continued for a
while to fulfill his duties under the king of Sweden as assessor
of the Bureau of Mines and a member of the House of Peers.
But in pursuing both his old and new life, his heart was split in
two. So, in 1747, when he was 59 years old, he resigned from
his thirty years of service to the king in the Bureau of Mines.

Holding his service in high regard, the king tried to promote him in rank, but he adamantly declined. The king still gave him half of his yearly salary after retirement. Swedenborg said, "There is no other reason for my resignation now than to newly exhaust all my strength in fulfilling a mission received from the Lord. When I retired from my post, the king told me of his intention to promote me in rank, but fearing the extent of my egotistical mind, I could not accept this."[26]

Swedenborg's first masterpiece, after embarking upon his spiritual career, was the great work *Arcana Coelestia*, a record of heavenly mysteries transmitted from God, as well as his own observations. Publishing the first volume in London in 1749, he completed the work in 1756. It consists of eight, large quarto volumes with 10,837 sections.[27] Containing about ten million words, and leaving nothing out, it delves in minute detail into the spiritual meaning of the first two books of the Old Testament, Genesis and Exodus. Throughout his commentary, Swedenborg unreservedly praises the learning, aspirations, beliefs, and people depicted therein. John Lewis published these mysterious volumes and was instructed by Swedenborg to keep the author's name a strict secret. According to the publisher, it took a whole year for Swedenborg to write the first volume. With hard work and diligence, Swedenborg produced more and more manuscripts, and upon publication, paid £200 out of his own pocket. When the second volume was issued, he again paid £200 to cover the bookseller's expenses. However, he did not take one penny of the profits for himself; all of it was donated to an association to propagate the Bible. Incidentally, all of Swedenborg's philosophical and religious works were written in Latin.

One thing that should be noted here is that, despite producing such a tremendous work, Swedenborg continued to fulfill his duties as a member of the House of Peers by voicing, without any hesitation, his commanding views on Sweden's public finances and administration. These opinions were not the vague, fanciful, and abstract statements commonly made by scholars and religious thinkers. His concrete plans always cut to the heart of the evils of his day.

After publishing this great work *[Arcana Coelestia]*, Swedenborg spent fifteen years—starting in 1756, when he was 68 years old—successively publishing his writings as if following a grand scheme. In 1758 *Heaven and Hell* appeared. This is a record of Swedenborg's firsthand encounters in heaven and hell and tells of such things as the structure, management, disposition, and population of these realms (originally published in London, 272 pages in quarto). The Japanese version of this book was published in 1910.[28] Those who want to know about Swedenborg's views on religion and spirituality must certainly read it. The Japanese translation is in small type and is a bulky volume of over 500 pages. It is written in a fairly inaccessible style, but thoughtful people will gain insights from reading through it. After giving its profound philosophy a careful reading, one naturally finds certain points agreeable, even though the work is initially intimidating. Those who seek the Way require perseverance.[29] I present the table of contents to allow a glimpse of the book's general features:

Heaven
Preface
The God of Heaven Is the Lord
It Is the Divine of the Lord That Makes Heaven
In Heaven the Divine of the Lord Is Love to Him and Charity
    toward the Neighbor
Heaven Is Divided into Two Kingdoms
There Are Three Heavens
The Heavens Consist of Innumerable Societies
Each Society Is a Heaven in a Smaller Form, and Each Angel
    in the Smallest Form
All Heaven in the Aggregate Reflects a Single Man

This list gives a picture of the kind of book *Heaven and Hell* is. To all appearances, it seems rather absurd; but those who have the enthusiasm, fortitude, and courage to give it a careful reading will eventually be rewarded. A sampling of Swedenborg's writings is included at the end of this book, giving the reader a fair understanding of his work. Here I would like to cite one passage: a timeless maxim pronounced by Swedenborg in *Heaven and Hell*, which says, "Will, namely love, makes the man" *(Voluntas aut amor sit ipse homo)*. A synopsis of paragraph 474 provides an explanation:[31]

> [I]t is the will that makes the man, while thought makes the man only so far as it goes forth from the will . . . or what is the same, it is love that makes the man, and faith only so far as it goes forth from love. Consequently, the will or love is the man himself. . . . It is not faith, but mere knowledge, which has no spiritual life in it. Even though false love may give the appearance of life, it is actually spiritual death, not life.[32]

The Last Judgment and the Destruction of Babylon shows how all the prophecies of the book of Revelation in the New Testament were realized in Swedenborg's life (originally published in London, 55 pages in quarto).[33] The commentary on the *White Horse [De Equo Albo]* is an excerpt from the *Arcana Coelestia*. It deals with the "white horse" of Revelation 19, minutely explaining the text and its spiritual significance (originally published in London, 23 pages in quarto). *Earths in Our Solar System* describes the conditions of various worlds, and the people, spirits, and angels who dwell in them (originally published in London, 72 pages in quarto).[34]

The New Jerusalem and Its Heavenly Doctrine contains Swedenborg's views on theology. Considered to have been discovered by him in heaven, these are the articles of belief informing the Swedenborgian church. The book interprets references to a new Jerusalem and a new heaven and earth at the beginning of Revelation 21 (originally published in London, 156 pages in quarto).[35]

This book will also appear in Japanese in the not-too-distant future. Those who wish to know the general themes of Swedenborg's theology need to read it. These themes are: Good and Truth; Will and Understanding; Externals and Internals; Love in general; Loves of Self and the World; Love and Charity toward the Neighbor; Faith; Devotion; Conscience; Freedom; Merit; Repentance and Remission of Sins; Regeneration; Temptation; Baptism; Communion; the Resurrection; Heaven and Hell; the Church; the Sacred Scripture, or the Word; Divine Providence; the Lord; and the Governance of Church and Society. This book contains extremely brief explanations of the subjects listed above.

In 1763 (when Swedenborg was 75 years old), *Divine Love and Wisdom* was issued.[36] As both a philosophical and theological work, it differs from the descriptive works written earlier. It first states that the Divine consists of love and wisdom and, using this as a foundation, establishes the main points of Swedenborg's theology. Because this book is extremely important in studying Swedenborg, I will give a summary of it here.

The entire book is composed of five chapters, which are further subdivided into 422 sections. A quarto volume of 151 pages in length, it was published in Amsterdam. On the first page, Swedenborg teaches that human life is love and that this love is no different from God. Therefore, God is human life, and people are the recipients of this life. Also, there is a distinction in the Divine between *Esse* (being) and *Existere* (form). These are two, yet they are one. Love is being, wisdom is form, and love depends on wisdom as wisdom depends on love. The Divine is a combination of these. The Divine manifests itself in the spiritual world as a sun, whose heat is love and whose light is wisdom. The sun of our world depends on this spiritual sun. Receiving its living heat and living light, the natural sun gives rise to all creation and makes it flourish. The purpose of the creation of the universe is to return all things to their origin in the Lord of creation, or the Divine, and thus establish a correspondence and conjunction between them.

The third chapter is an analysis of degrees, Swedenborg's unique philosophy by which he explains the order of creation and the progress of the spirit. At once simultaneous and successive, discrete and continuous, the degrees of length and breadth are each divided into three parts. In making sense of Swedenborg's theology, it is necessary to understand his analysis of degrees. Next, he discusses the rationality and freedom of the human mind, saying that evil results from damage to these two forces.

In the fourth chapter, he teaches that the eternal God created the universe and all things within it from himself, and not from nothing.[37] He says that the true purpose of creation is the realization of "uses" for each of its manifold forms and concludes that uses progressively turn into the forms of creation. Within Swedenborg's philosophy of use are many points that deserve close attention.

The fifth chapter is on psychology. According to Swedenborg, the human mind derives from will and understanding. The will receives the divine love and understanding receives the divine wisdom, both of them forming human life. Life, in its first principles, is in the brain and, in its derivatives, in the body. From these first principles, life is transmitted into its derivatives; and from these derivatives, life is gathered into the first principles. Therefore, it is the nature of our love that determines the character of our understanding and personality. In short, love makes the man. When, based on the principle of correspondence, the relationship between wisdom and love is applied to the body, the will becomes the heart and the understanding, the lungs. The operation of the body by the lungs and heart is like the dependence of the human mind on will

and understanding (in regard to this, Swedenborg gives an
analysis of breath, for there seems to be a close relationship
between the regulation of the breath and the activity of the
spirit. Please consult his own discussion of his experiments).[38]
His explanation of the relationship of both is extremely thorough, extending finally to the relation between faith and charity. The publication of this book in Japanese is not far off.

In the same year that *Divine Love and Wisdom* was published, or 1763, the new Swedenborgian teachings were published in four separate books on the themes of "the Lord,"
"the Sacred Scripture," "Life," and "Faith" (published in Amsterdam in quarto, these four books combined come to 177
pages).[39] In 1764, when Swedenborg was 76 years old, *Divine
Providence* appeared. This work is another philosophical explanation of his theology and is of the same importance as the
earlier *Divine Love and Wisdom*. It was published in Amsterdam (quarto volume containing 214 pages divided into 18
chapters, with 340 subheadings).[40]

The major theme of *Divine Providence* is that the purpose
of the universe, which is governed by a divine providence
based on divine love and divine wisdom, is to establish a
heaven from human beings. In discussing the laws of divine
providence, Swedenborg includes an argument on free will,
saying that providence causes people to act of their free will,
according to the faculty of reason. Therefore, from a human
standpoint, it seems we lack restraint, that we are unregulated,
without impetus. On our own, evil is eliminated and good encouraged. We feel as if there is nothing that does not depend
on our own faculties. But, in fact, this is not to say that nothing depends on the power of the Divine, only that the extent of
divine providence is thereby unknown to people. Divine providence does not seek to restrain the human mind from without, for again, it does not wish anyone to be conscious of its
influence. However, God asks that we humans seek out the

truth of the divine providence. This truth is universal, there being no place where it does not reach. Therefore, it is not subject to human calculations, and no matter what the roll of the die, everything completely derives from divine providence, which extends through eternity, determining everything before it happens. However, people are not able to know this. The mysterious workings of providence are not perceived by ordinary folk. All that people can do is to exhaust their faculty of reason and to exercise the power of their freedom, entrusting what remains to the workings of heaven. In this way, Swedenborg tried to skillfully harmonize the arguments for predestination and free will.

Swedenborg next discusses in this book the relationship between understanding and will, saying that things that enter only into the understanding and not the will are like froth on water. Because they stop at the surface of one's mind and do not penetrate its core, they do not result in outward action. No matter how much someone's understanding advances, when it is not accompanied by feeling, it will hinder that person's spiritual progress. Therefore, people must first purify their feelings and seek out those things in the will that are good.

Next, Swedenborg explains the reason there is evil and falsehood in the world. This section resembles the Buddhist teaching of expedient means.[41] That is, it is divine providence that allows evil and falsehood to strut about temporarily in order that they may be overcome by good and truth. This is not to say that providence does not manifest itself in both good and evil people. Divine providence is continually inviting people to enter heaven. People are free to respond to this and do good and are also free not to respond and do evil. Evil use of this freedom results from attachment to the self *(proprium)*.[42] Each person has the predisposition and capacity to be saved; and not being saved, or falling from grace, comes from not saving oneself. The road to salvation entails recognizing vari-

ous evils as sins against divine providence and shunning them.
Therefore, doing an evil act again and again after recognizing
it as evil is an offense against providence. It is not enough to
say that you have committed an evil; you must perceive its
greater religious significance and avoid it to the best of your
ability while tending only toward good. This is the quickest
route to salvation. Salvation comes gradually; it is not immediately actualized through the direct grace of God, for this is
contrary to divine providence. By faith alone salvation is impossible; we must acknowledge that not until charity and love
are added is the fruit of salvation born. Passing through a lifetime committing sins, even if you say on your deathbed, "I beg
you, God, save me," this will not in one stroke wash clean the
stain of the previous years. From the start, it is crucial to have
a penitent heart and, recognizing one's sins, to accumulate
good deeds as befit love and wisdom. In this way, a peaceful
death is attained. These are the main features of *Divine Providence*. This book will probably be published [in Japanese] after *Divine Love and Wisdom* has already come out, and Swedenborg scholars will certainly need to read it.

Apocalypse Revealed [Apocalypsis Revelata] was issued in
1766, when Swedenborg reached the age of 78. In this work,
he unveiled the secret meaning of the book of Revelation,
which has traditionally been attributed to John. Describing
things that he experienced in a spiritual vision, his statements
are extremely fantastic and shifting, and perplex the reader as
to their meaning. Swedenborg considered this work, that is, its
spiritual meaning, to have been transmitted by angels (published in Amsterdam, 629 pages in quarto).

In 1768, the book *Conjugial Love* appeared.[43] Swedenborg
was 80 at the time. This work expounds on both purity and
impurity in love between the sexes. That which is pure arises
from heartfelt love and binds the two sexes, harmonizing the
husband's intelligence and the wife's affection. That which is

impure manifests itself as mere external union and is perverse. This book is divided into two parts containing 535 sections (published in Amsterdam, 328 pages in quarto).

A Brief Exposition of the Doctrine of the New Church [Summaria Expositio Doctrinae Novae Ecclesiae] was published in 1769. It relates in simple terms the doctrine of the new church advocated by Swedenborg and clarifies the meaning of the "new Jerusalem" in Revelation (published in Amsterdam, 67 pages in quarto). In the same year, a small pamphlet called *The Interaction of the Soul and the Body* was issued in London.[44]

In 1771, when he was 83 years old, Swedenborg published his last work, *True Christian Religion [Vera Christiana Religio]*, in which he systematically explains his theology. First discussing absolute reality, he goes on to speak of the Savior's teachings and follows this with fourteen chapters: the Holy Spirit, the Trinity, the Sacred Scripture, the Exoteric and Esoteric Significance of the Ten Commandments, Faith, Love, Free Will, Repentance, Reformation, Regeneration, Remission of Sins, Baptism, Communion, the End of the Church, the Lord's Coming, the New Heaven, and the New Church. This huge book consists of 851 sections.

True Christian Religion was the last work that Swedenborg published. On March 29 (a Sunday) of the following year, 1772, he announced in a London boarding house the termination of his life in this world. He was 84 years old. Besides his published books, Swedenborg left a number of manuscripts. For example, he preserved the details of his spiritual encounters in his *Spiritual Diary*, extending from 1747 to [1765].[45] From the publication of *Apocalypse Revealed* in 1766, he mentioned his experiences as "articles to be remembered" in each of his works. They had all been previously collected into the *Spiritual Diary*; however, a great many are not available to the general reader.[46] These manuscripts have been photolithographed one by one, and exist in the original text (in Latin). The manuscripts are folded into two and the characters are very small; they are orderly and exquisite to behold. An old man in his seventies and eighties, every day ardently at work on his writing, leaving his country for Holland and England to get it published, not knowing a day's peace: when today's lazy scholars think of this, they feel like crawling into a hole.

There was apparently a very strong bond between Swedenborg and England,[47] one not limited to the two or three visits he made to England to study abroad and publish, for it seems that he actually came to London with the intention of departing from this world. He made his final crossing to England in the summer of 1771, after he had published *True Christian Religion* in Amsterdam; and in March of the following year, he abandoned his earthly body in a London boarding house. He knew of his death beforehand, informing the proprietress and maid. They said that, in watching the approach of his death, Swedenborg was as delighted as a child who was going off to a festival or out to play. During his lifetime, this old man of 84 years had already witnessed conditions in the other world. He had a personal and thorough knowledge of where he would go. So, knowing that he would at last enter this region, why should he not be pleased?

His body was buried in London in a cemetery affiliated with the Swedish church; but in 1908 (the same time that I was in England), after 136 years had elapsed, the king of Sweden endorsed the National Academy's wish to have Swedenborg's body moved back to his homeland. It was transported by the Swedish navy and reburied at the Cathedral in Uppsala. In order to memorialize him, [the Swedish] Parliament erected a marble sarcophagus. The nation's great figures are buried at Uppsala Cathedral, which can be compared with England's Westminster Abbey.

CHAPTER 4

A Singular Spiritual Vision

In contemporary Japan, there has been a lot of commotion surrounding psychological research into clairvoyance and clairvoyants. Should we not say that someone like Swedenborg provides excellent material for this research? Making personal circuits of heaven and hell, he discussed their organization in tangible terms, including descriptions of angels, spirits, devils, and other residents dwelling there. This alone, viewed from the standpoint of psychology, makes him a figure requiring thorough investigation. In addition, he presents other questions concerning religion and philosophy. His clairvoyant abilities and his power to view the past would be particularly good research topics for psychologists. Swedenborg could have used his spiritual powers to gain fame and fortune, had he so desired. There appears to be evidence, difficult to disprove, that he truly had this kind of mysterious, spiritual communication. However, in fulfilling his noble life's work, he did not display to others such coarse abilities. Even though people came and asked him to demonstrate his powers, he did not readily acquiesce, saying that a rapport with the realm of the dead could be granted only by the Lord God. He said that, unless it were an emergency, he could not enter a [spiritual] exchange. Since it was the existence of divine providence, in its profundity, that discriminated the path between this world and the next, it could not be recklessly attempted through the faculties of ordinary people. He also said that what allowed for his interaction with the spirit world was the fact that God had given commands expressly to him and that there was nothing at all exotic about this. To vainly please the hearts of worldly folk would be to forget the purpose of his mission. The divine will did not lie here, he said.

Of course, this kind of statement might seem like pretense. The general reader naturally desires proof of Swedenborg's so-called clairvoyant abilities. Therefore, I will provide an example that will not allow any doubts to remain: an exhaustive investigation made by Immanuel Kant, a contemporary of Swedenborg, in the name of psychological research. In a letter dated August 10, 1758 (but actually written in 1768), Kant informed Charlotte Von Knobloch:[48]

> The following occurrence appears to me to have the greatest weight of proof, and to place the assertion respecting Swedenborg's extraordinary gift beyond all possibility of doubt. In September of 1756 (it actually occurred in July of 1759), on Saturday at four o'clock, p.m., Swedenborg arrived at Gothenburg from England, when Mr. William Castel invited him to his house together with a party of fifteen persons. About six o'clock, Swedenborg went out, and returned to the company quite pale and alarmed. He said that a dangerous fire had just broken out in the southern district of Stockholm (about 300 English miles from Gothenburg), and that it was spreading very fast. He was restless, and went out often. He said that the house of one of his friends, whom he named, was already in ashes, and that his own was in danger. At eight o'clock, after he had been out again, he joyfully exclaimed, "Thank God! The fire is extinguished, the third door from my house." This news occasioned great commotion throughout the whole city, but particularly amongst the company in which he was. It was announced to the governor the same evening. On Sunday

morning, Swedenborg was summoned to the governor, who questioned him concerning the disaster. Swedenborg described the fire precisely, how it had begun, and in what manner it had ceased, and how long it had continued. On the same day the news spread through the city, and as the governor had thought it worthy of attention the consternation was considerably increased; because many were in trouble on account of their friends and property, which might have been involved in the disaster. On Monday evening a messenger arrived at Gothenburg, who was dispatched by the Board of Trade during the time of the fire. In the letters brought by him the fire was described precisely in the manner stated by Swedenborg. On Tuesday morning the royal courier arrived at the governor's, with the melancholy intelligence of the fire, of the loss which it had occasioned, and of the houses it had damaged and ruined, not in the least differing from that which Swedenborg had given at the very time when it had happened, for the fire was extinguished at eight o'clock.[49]

There are further occurrences that attest to the singularity of Swedenborg's spiritual vision, but since these sorts of things will not raise or lower estimations of his true character, I will not prattle on about them now. I wish to conclude only by noting that he had these sorts of experiences.

CHAPTER 5

Character and Lifestyle

As for Swedenborg's appearance, there is no reliable documentation to which we can refer. We know how he looked only from his portraits, and it seems there are not many good ones. One was painted for Swedenborg's close friend Count Anders J. von Höpken, with the original hanging in the Gripsholm National Museum Of Art.[50] You see the wisdom that abounds in his features and sense the prudence and steadfastness of his will. In particular, you see in the glint of his eyes a dignity and magical power, and know he is not an ordinary man.

In his latter years, Swedenborg had a friend in Amsterdam named John Christian Cuno, who, although not a devotee of Swedenborg, was captivated by his personality. Cuno left a very interesting account of him, saying, ". . . when he gazed on me with his smiling blue eyes—as he always did in conversing—it was as if truth itself was speaking from them."[51] It seems that, when faced with these eyes, even those who jeered at him were filled with awe. Cuno also said:

> I often noticed with surprise how scoffers, who had made their way into large societies where I had taken him, and whose purpose it had been to make fun of the old gentleman, forgot all their laughter and their intended scoffing, and how they stood agape and listened to the most singular things which he like an

open-hearted child told about the spiritual world without re-
serve and with full confidence. It almost seemed as if his eyes
possessed the faculty of imposing silence on every one.[52]

When one claims to have already toured heaven and hell, to
have received direct orders from the Lord God, and so forth,
it is only human nature to hold oneself up high arrogantly, or
to be intolerant, harsh, and incompatible with others. But
Swedenborg was the complete opposite of this. He was childlike and innocent in all matters, with the air of a transcendent
mystic who had escaped defilement. Count von Höpken said:

> I have not only known him these two-and-forty years, but also,
> some time since, daily frequented his company[53]. . . . I do not
> recollect to have known any man of more uniformly virtuous
> character than Swedenborg; always contented, never fretful or
> morose. . . . He was a true philosopher and lived like one. He
> labored diligently, and lived frugally. . . . He possessed a sound
> judgment upon all occasions . . . and expressed himself well on
> every subject.[54]
>
> [He strongly rejected worldly philosophers. He was a model
> of sincerity, virtue and piety, and from what I have seen, there
> is no one in my country possessing as profound a knowledge
> as that of Swedenborg.][55]

Swedenborg's lifestyle was extremely simple, in accordance
with his principal occupation. In regard to his life in Amsterdam, Cuno said:

> He lived with simple burgher folks, who kept a shop in which
> they sold chintz, muslin, handkerchiefs, and the like, and who
> had quite a number of little children. I inquired of the landlady
> whether the old gentleman did not require very much atten-
> tion. She answered, "He scarcely requires any; the servant has
> nothing else to do for him, except in the morning to lay the fire
> in the fireplace. Every evening he goes to bed at seven, and gets

up in the morning at eight. We do not trouble ourselves any more about him. During the day he keeps up the fire himself; and on going to bed he takes great care, lest the fire should do any damage. He dresses and undresses himself alone, and waits upon himself in everything, so that we scarcely know whether there is any one in the house or not. I should like him to be with us for the rest of his life. My children will miss him most; for he never goes out without bringing them home some sweets; the little rogues also dote upon the old gentleman so much, that they prefer him to their own parents. I imagine that he is very rich . . . ."[56]

At this time, Swedenborg was already over 80 years old. Although an old man in his seventies and eighties, he crossed the ocean alone, traveling from Sweden to Holland and England without any companion. That was a different age from today; he did not have the convenience of trains and steamships. Even crossing from England to Holland with a favorable wind took over a week's time, so that far and wide people sang about the troubles of the journey. Yet this vigorous old mystic bounced from one port to another, and thought of nothing but publishing the works he believed he had written under heaven's orders.

As Milton said, "To share in sacred meals with the gods, one must eat modestly."[57] Indeed, it seems that gluttony and spiritual discipline cannot coexist. Swedenborg always warned against being overcome by bodily desire, as evil energy exudes from the pores of those who indulge in a lavish diet, and this intent gives rise to maggots and worms that fill the room. When he first began having his spiritual experiences, the quality of his food was no different from that of ordinary people, and he merely refrained from taking more than small portions. But during the last fifteen years of his life, he hardly ever ate meat, and only occasionally ate fish, usually eel. His main meals were limited to bread, butter, milk, coffee, almonds, raisins, vegetables, biscuits, cake, and gingerbread. He would always distribute sweets among small children. He also drank a lot of water and especially liked coffee. It seems there is a very close relationship between philosophers and caffeine. Even in Japan's case, tea was first imported from China through Buddhist monks; and since then, a special bond has developed between Buddhist priests and tea.

Swedenborg was greatly fond of snuff, and today particles of it still remain among his manuscripts, exuding a lingering smell. Because of this smell, curiously enough, his manuscripts have escaped damage from bookworms. Although we cannot go so far as to call him a vegetarian, he did not have much of a liking for meat, and it appears he recognized that a taste for meat tended to be contrary to the way of heaven. He said:

> People in very ancient times did not eat meat, for they considered killing animals to be atrocious. But later, as time passed, people's hearts grew cruel and brutal. They came to think nothing of slaughtering living creatures and eating their flesh. As long as human beings possess this character, I suppose it is impossible for them to stop eating meat.[58]

It seems that eating meat is incompatible with pure and lofty thoughts.

Swedenborg's dress was very simple, with no adornments to attract the eyes of others, but that was quite suitable for someone of his character. When he went out, according to the custom of the time, he wore a wig, but it was not very long. At his waist he wore a sword in a strange sheath, and in his hand he carried a cane with a gold head. On his feet he wore shoes whose buckles were adorned with silver and gold, and inlaid with jewels. Granted, silver, gold, and jewels might seem rather ostentatious; but for people in Swedenborg's station at the time, these were not especially remarkable. Moreover, as the end of his life approached, it is said his heart became so completely absorbed in his calling that, when he went out, there might be something strange about his costume; and that when there was no one around to put it right, he would walk into the crowds without noticing it. One time, he went somewhere in response to an invitation but wore shoes with mismatched buckles. When he arrived at the house, the young ladies there reportedly laughed at him.

As Swedenborg grew older, he became completely oblivious to such things as what the date might be, or whether it was day or night, and worked diligently on his writings. He went to bed whenever he felt sleepy, without regard to a fixed time. Once, he slept for thirteen hours without waking. When he entered a kind of meditative state, he would lie in bed for days without eating and working. When his death was not far off, he immersed himself in this sort of meditation for three or four weeks, not taking any nourishment. Afterward, Swedenborg got up and returned to his former self, or so it is reported. In these instances, he allowed no one to approach, saying that he must arise naturally by himself. When he woke up from this type of sleep, he would immediately kindle the fire and take up his pen.

His indifference to money is a documented fact. In addition to his pension from the Swedish government, he had a fair number of assets; the interest provided for his daily life, travels, and publishing expenses. Because he already had this income, he took no profits from his publications and did not plan any other money-making ventures. In this regard, he fortunately had gained a great deal of independence.

He also did not care for loans and detested almsgiving, saying, "The world's beggars, when they are not lazy, are ruffians. Even if they are pitiable, when you do not investigate them and give indiscriminately, you actually fail them."[59] This is certainly sound reasoning. Today's philanthropy is based on this principle, so that individuals do not give alms on the street, and money and goods are not the only things offered.

According to Swedenborg's thinking, lending money was tantamount to losing money. Moreover, since he needed all of his income for his travels and publishing, he did not finance other people, and he also did not take on debt. But although he budgeted carefully, when the landlord asked for his rent, he had the man go to the place where Swedenborg kept his purse and take the amount required as he pleased. In addition, all those who had financial dealings with him said he was generous.

The number of works written by Swedenborg over sixty-three years is surprisingly large. If all of them were put in octavo volumes of 500 pages each, it would come to 60 volumes. However, this is actually not all of his work, for there are also unpublished manuscripts located in the National Library in Stockholm, many of which are being researched by scholars. All of them deal with very profound thoughts, and are not products of one night's hasty work. Of course, in places, it seems as if the same points are repeated again and again; but the fact that Swedenborg could not desist—pressed as he was to meet the demands of divine revelation—does not detract from the quality of his writing as a whole. This is because his elder brother-in-law, Bishop Benzelius, trained him to be very economical with his time. If it were not for this, he would not have been able to produce works so rich in both quality and quantity.

Also surprising is the fact that he wrote all of his works completely by himself, without the assistance of a secretary or copyist. Each volume is orderly and systematic, without one line out of place. He set up a sort of index right from the beginning, so when he wrote a book, any references or citations to previously published sections were well-organized and free of mistakes. This index was also compiled into one large volume, giving those who look at it an understanding of just how many dictums Swedenborg bequeathed. Abbé Anton Joseph Pernety said, "Swedenborg was an indefatigible man who wrote day and night."[60] Cuno said in his memoirs:

> [H]e labours in a most astonishing and superhuman manner at his new work. Sixteen sheets, in type twice as small as those used in his former works, are already printed. . . . for every printed sheet he has to fill four sheets in manuscript. He now has two sheets printed every week. These he corrects himself; and consequently he has to write eight sheets every week.[61]

This was certainly industrious, for at this point, Swedenborg was just three days short of 83 years. Although people say Swedenborg's work was wild and confused, that was certainly not the case. When it came to important matters, he would revise his drafts a number of times; and if the results were not satisfactory, he would throw them away and not look at them again. After entering old age, because he spent much of his time traveling—or, rather, since there was no need for them—he did not carry even one reference work, making only a portion of the Hebrew scriptures his library.

Swedenborg's works on religion were published in England and Holland, but not in his homeland; for at the time, only the former two countries possessed freedom of religion. At first he thought he would print *True Christian Religion* in Paris; but when he petitioned the censor's bureau, he was told that if, "as always," he indicated under the title that it was published in London or Amsterdam, the book could be published in Paris. Even in such a small matter, Swedenborg did not wish to deceive the world, so taking the book to Amsterdam, he had it printed there.

I would like to share one final story concerning his character and conduct, as told by the Swedish historian Anders Fryxell:

My grandmother, when she was a girl of fifteen or sixteen, lived with her father not far from Swedenborg's house, and was thus on friendly terms with him. My grandmother, the young lady, was impelled by her childlike curiosity, and often asked "Uncle Swedenborg" to show her a spirit or angel. At last he consented, and leading her to a summer-house in his garden, he placed her before a curtain . . . and then said, "Now you shall see an angel!" and as he spoke, he drew up the curtain, when the young lady beheld herself reflected in a mirror.[62]

CHAPTER 6

General Views and Statements

As for Swedenborg's experiences of visiting heaven and hell, the purpose of the present book is not to argue whether they truly derived from the hidden will of the Lord God or not. At any rate, it seems that these experiences of Swedenborg's were closely related to his breathing, causing him to perform extensive research into the art of respiration. According to his theory of "correspondence," the lungs of the human body correspond to understanding, and the heart corresponds to love. Since the spiritual connection between love and understanding is the same as that between the heart and lungs, if you know one, then you can discern the other. Correct regulation of the breath, therefore, advances understanding. In breathing, there is a distinction between internal and external, with external breath coming from the mundane world and internal breath from the spiritual world. When people die, their external breath ceases. However, the tranquil and soundless inner breath continues endlessly. While people are still in a corporeal state, it is difficult for them to feel their internal breath, because it is tranquil. This breath, which arises entirely from the true faith possessed by the spirit, is the life of the spirit. Accordance with the spiritual world depends on this breath.

Swedenborg discussed his personal experience of this breathing:

I was first accustomed thus to feel my internal breath in my early childhood, when saying my morning and evening prayers, and occasionally afterwards, when exploring the harmonies of the lungs and heart, and especially when deeply engaged in writing philosophical works. For a course of years I continually observed that there was a tacit respiration, scarcely perceptible, concerning which it was subsequently given me to reflect, and then to write. I was thus from the period of childhood able to stop my external breathing and activate only my internal breath, especially by means of absorbing speculations, as otherwise the intense study of truth is scarcely possible. Afterwards, when heaven was opened to me, and I was enabled to converse with spirits, I scarcely breathed by inspiration at all for the space of an hour.[63]

Although not all of us can perceive the distinction between external and internal breath in the way Swedenborg did, there is doubtless a close relation between regulation of the breath and cultivation of the mind and body. The fact that Swedenborg could feel this almost from birth probably holds some significance for the mission of his later years.

Having attained the spiritual realm, Swedenborg set out to inform his readers about the things he had observed there. Looking at the chapter titles in *Heaven and Hell,* we discover these observations throughout, but now I should give one or two examples. The first comes from section 232 in *Conjugial Love,* the second relation in "Universals concerning Marriage" (see also section 333 in *True Christian Religion*):

After some time I again heard from the lower earth, as before, the cries "O how learned!" and "O how wise!" And I looked around to see what angels were then present, and lo! those were there who were from the heaven immediately over them that were crying "O how learned!" And I spoke to them about the cry. They said, "These 'learned' are they that merely reason whether a thing is or is not, and rarely think that it is so, and therefore are like winds that blow and pass away, or like barks upon trees without a heart, or as shells of almonds without any kernel, or rinds upon fruits with no pulp. For their minds are without interior judgment and are united with the bodily senses only. If therefore the very senses do not judge, they can form no conclusion. In a word they are merely sensual, and by us are called 'reasoners' because they never come to any conclusion but take up whatever they hear and discuss whether it is, by perpetually contradicting. And they like nothing more than to attack very truths, and so by bringing them into dispute to tear them in pieces. These are they who believe themselves learned above all in the world."

Hearing these things I asked the angels to conduct me to them. And they brought me to a cavern from which steps led down to the lower earth. We descended and followed the cry "O how learned!" and behold, some hundreds were standing in one place beating the ground with their feet.

Surprised at this at first, I asked, "Why do they thus stand and beat the ground with the soles of their feet?" and said "They may thus hollow out the ground with their feet." At this the angels smiled and said, "They appear to stand thus, because they do not think concerning anything that it is so, but only think and discuss whether it is, and as the thought makes no further progress they appear merely to tread and grind a single clod, and not to advance." But then I went toward this congregation, and lo! they appeared to me men of not unhandsome face and in comely raiment. But the angels said, "In their own light they thus appear, but if light from heaven flows in, their faces, and their garments also, change." And it was so. They then appeared with swarthy countenances, and clothed in black sack-cloth. But when this light was withdrawn, they appeared as before.

Presently I spoke to some of them and said, "I heard the multitude about you shouting 'O how learned!' May I then be permitted some conversation with you, to discuss subjects of profoundest erudition?"

They answered, "Say whatever you please and we will satisfy you."

And I asked, "What must the religion be whereby a man is saved?"

They replied, "We must divide the question into several, and cannot give answer until we have formed a conclusion upon them. The first consideration must be, Whether religion is anything? The second, Whether there is salvation or not? The third, Whether one religion is more effective than another? The fourth, Whether there is a heaven, and a hell? And fifth, Whether there is eternal life after death? Besides others."

I asked about the first question, "Whether religion is anything?" And they began to discuss it, with abundance of arguments as to whether there is religion, and whether what is called so is anything. And I begged that they would refer it to the congregation, and they referred it. And the common response was that this proposition required so much investigation that it could not be finished within the evening.

I asked, "Can you finish it within a year?" And one said it could not be done within a hundred years.

I replied, "Meanwhile you are without religion."

And he responded, "Should it not first be shown whether there is religion, whether what is so-called is anything? If it is, it must be for the wise also. If not, then it must be only for the common people. It is known that religion is called a bond; but it is asked, 'For whom?' If only for the common people, in itself it is nothing. If also for the wise it is something."

Hearing these things I said to them, "You are anything but learned, for you are only able to think whether a thing is, and to turn it this way and that. Who can become learned unless he knows something for certain, and goes forward in that as a man advances from step to step, and so on successively into wisdom. Otherwise you do not so much as touch truths with the fingernail, but put them more and more out of sight. To reason only whether a thing is, is it not like arguing about a cap which is never put on? or a shoe that is never worn? What comes of it except that you do not know whether there is anything? That is to say, Whether there is salvation? Whether there is eternal life after death? Whether one religion is more effective than another? Whether there is a heaven and a hell? You cannot think of anything about these things so long as you stick fast in the first step and beat the sand there, and do not set foot beyond foot and go forward. Beware lest your minds, while they stand thus without outside of judgment, grow hard within and become statues of salt, and you, friends of Lot's wife."

Having said this I went away, and they in indignation threw stones after me. And then they appeared to me like graven images of stone, wherein there is nothing of human reason. I asked the angels respecting their lot; and they said, "Their lot is that they are let down into the deep, and into a desert there, and are set to carrying packs; and then being unable to bring forth anything from reason, they chatter and talk nonsense. And from a distance they appear then like asses bearing burdens."[64]

I do not know whether or not Swedenborg saw the fate of the so-called scholars in the spiritual world, but his words pierce the heart like a sharp knife. In the end, are learned people asses bearing burdens?

Swedenborg's spiritual visions are not all like this, and I present it only as one example. Sensitive readers will perceive that this story contains a logic that only seems illogical, that what seems absurd is actually rich in common sense and in accord with human nature and everyday experience. As for its significance, we must say that Swedenborg is a great and unique critic.

In order to know Swedenborg, one must first know *Heaven and Hell*. His theological teachings, or what he attempted to transmit to human beings through his heavenly mission, concern the existence of a spiritual world. I will now cite some of his assertions on this matter:

As there are infinite varieties in heaven, and no one society nor any one angel is exactly like any other, there are in heaven general, specific and particular divisions. The general division is into two kingdoms, the specific into three heavens, and the particular into innumerable societies. Each of these will be treated of in what follows. The general division is said to be into kingdoms, because heaven is called "the kingdom of God."

There are angels that receive more interiorly the Divine that goes forth from the Lord, and others that receive it less interiorly; the former are called celestial angels, and the latter spiritual angels. Because of this difference heaven is divided into two kingdoms, one called the Celestial Kingdom, the other the Spiritual Kingdom.

As the angels that constitute the celestial kingdom receive the Divine of the Lord more interiorly they are called interior and also higher angels; and for the same reason the heavens that they constitute are called interior and higher heavens. They are called higher and lower, because these terms designate what is interior and what is exterior.

The love in which those are, who are in the celestial kingdom is called celestial love, and the love in which those are who are in the spiritual kingdom is called spiritual love. Celestial love is love to the Lord, and spiritual love is love towards the neighbor. And as all good pertains to love (for good to any one is what he loves) the good also of the one kingdom is called celestial, and the good of the other spiritual. Evidently, then, the two kingdoms are distinguished from each other in the same way as good of love to the Lord is distinguished from good of love towards the neighbor. And as the good of love to the Lord is an interior good, and that love is interior love, so the celestial angels are interior angels, and are called higher angels.

(HH 20–23)

That there is light in the heavens those who think from nature alone cannot comprehend; and yet such is the light in the heavens that it exceeds by many degrees the noonday light of the world. That light I have often seen, even during the evening and night. At first I wondered when I heard the angels say that the light of this world is little more than a shadow in comparison with the light of heaven; but having seen it I can testify that it is so. The brightness and splendor of the light of heaven are such as cannot be described. All things that I have seen in the heavens have been seen in that light, thus more clearly and distinctly than things in this world. (HH 126)

But it is better to present the evidence of experience. Whenever I have talked with angels face to face, I have been with them in their abodes. These abodes are precisely like abodes on the earth which we call houses, but more beautiful. In them there are chambers, parlors, and bedrooms in great number; there are also courts, and there are gardens and flowerbeds and lawns round about. Where they live together their houses are near each other, arranged one next to the other in the form of a city, with avenues, streets, and public squares, exactly like cities on the earth. I have been permitted to pass through them, looking about on every side, and sometimes entering the houses. This occurred when my inner sight was opened, and I was fully awake. (*HH* 184)

I have seen palaces in heaven of such magnificence as cannot be described. Above they glittered as if made of pure gold, and below as if made of precious stones, some more splendid than others. It was the same within. Both words and knowledge are inadequate to describe the decorations that adorned the rooms. On the side looking to the south there were parks, where, too, every thing shone, in some places the leaves glistening as if made of silver, and fruit as if made of gold; while the flowers in their beds formed rainbows with their colors. Beyond the borders, where the view terminated, were seen other palaces. Such is the architecture of heaven that you would say that art there is in its art; and now wonder, because the art itself is from heaven. The angels said that such things and innumerable others still more perfect are presented before their eyes by the Lord; and yet these things are more pleasing to their minds than to their eyes, because in every one of them they see a correspondence, and through the correspondences what is Divine.   (*HH* 185)

In trying to judge the whole work from only the above passages on heaven and angels, one might misinterpret it. My purpose in using them here is to show what Swedenborg's attitude was toward recording circumstances in the realm of the dead. Readers need to be attentive and look at them again.

Next, as for what he said about hell:

> The way that leads to heaven and the way that leads to hell were once represented to me. There was a broad way tending towards the left or the north, and many spirits were seen going in it; but at a distance a large stone was seen where the broad way came to an end. From that stone two ways branched off, one to the left and one in the opposite direction to the right. The way that went to the left was narrow or straightened, leading through the west to the south, and thus into the light of heaven; the way that went to the right was broad and spacious, leading obliquely downwards towards hell. All at first seemed to be going the same way until they came to the large stone at the head of the two ways. When they reached that point they divided; the good turned to the left and entered the straightened way that led to heaven; while the evil, not seeing the stone at the fork of the ways fell upon it and were hurt; and when they rose up they ran on in the broad way to the right which went towards hell.   (*HH* 534)

> I have also been permitted to look into the hells and to see what they are within; for when the Lord wills, the sight of a spirit or angel from above may penetrate into the lowest depths beneath and explore their character, notwithstanding the coverings. In this way I have been permitted to look into them. Some of the hells appeared to the view like caverns and dens in rocks extending inward and then downward into an

abyss, either obliquely or vertically. Some of the hells appeared to the view like the dens and caves of wild beasts in forests; some like the hollow caverns and passages that are seen in mines, with caverns extending towards the lower regions. Most of the hells are threefold, the upper one appearing within to be in dense darkness, because inhabited by those who are in the falsities of evil; while the lower ones appear fiery, because inhabited by those who are in evils themselves, dense darkness corresponding to the falsities of evil, and fire to evils themselves. Those that have acted interiorly from evil are in the deeper hells, and those that have acted exteriorly from evil, that is, from the falsities of evil, are in the hells that are less deep. Some hells present an appearance like the ruins of houses and cities after conflagrations, in which infernal spirits dwell and hide themselves. In the milder hells there is an appearance of rude huts, in some cases contiguous in the form of a city with lanes and streets, and within the houses are infernal spirits engaged in unceasing quarrels, enmities, fightings, and brutalities; while in the streets and lanes robberies and depredations are committed. In some of the hells there are nothing but brothels, disgusting to the sight and filled with every kind of filth and excrement. Again, there are dark forests, in which infernal spirits roam like wild beasts and where, too, there are underground dens into which those flee who are pursued by others. There are also deserts, where all is barren and sandy, and where in some places there are ragged rocks in which there are caverns, and in some places huts. Into these desert places those are cast out from the hells who have suffered every extremity of punishment, especially those who in the world have been more cunning than others in undertaking and contriving intrigues and deceits. Such a life is their final lot.   (*HH* 586)

In order to understand correctly Swedenborg's vision of the spiritual world, we need to know about his doctrines of representation, correspondence, degrees, and influx. Since this book does not go into such depth, the reader must make a close study of *Heaven And Hell, Divine Love and Wisdom,* and *Divine Providence*. However, one thing to note here is that Swedenborg's heaven and hell are not conditioned by time and space, as they are a kind of spiritual state. Therefore, neither heaven nor hell exists apart from this world, although this world also does not equal heaven or hell. Perhaps we should say that the relationship between them [heaven and hell and the material world] is neither one of equivalence nor separation. When we consider that our spiritual lives have no beginning in time or space and that the circumstances of heaven and hell are produced from these lives, then clearly we should not take Swedenborg's statements literally. This is the basis for the doctrines of correspondence and representation. The reader should not form hasty opinions.

To demonstrate some of Swedenborg's teachings, I will provide selections from his work:

> That it is not so difficult to live the life of heaven as some believe can now be seen from this, that when any thing presents itself to a man that he knows to be dishonest and unjust, but to which his mind is borne, it is simply necessary for him to think that it ought not to be done because it is opposed to the divine precepts. If a man accustoms himself so to think, and from so doing establishes a habit of so thinking, he is gradually conjoined to heaven; and so far as he is conjoined to heaven the higher regions of his mind are opened; and so far as these are opened he sees whatever is dishonest and unjust, and so far as he sees these evils they can be dispersed, for no evil can be dispersed until it is seen. Into this state man is able to enter because of his freedom, for is not any one able from his freedom to so think? And when man has made a beginning the Lord quickens all that is good in him, and causes him not only to see evils to be evils, but also to refrain from willing them, and finally to turn away from them. This is meant by the Lord's words, "My yoke is easy and My burden is light" (Matthew 11:30). But it must be understood that the difficulty of so thinking and of resisting evils increases so far as man from his

will does evils, for in the same measure he becomes accustomed to them until he no longer sees them, and at length loves them and from the delight of his love excuses them, and confirms them by every kind of fallacy, and declares them to be allowable and good. This is the fate of those who in early youth plunge into evils without restraint, and also reject Divine things from the heart. (HH 533)

What love of self is can be seen by comparing it with heavenly love. Heavenly love consists in loving uses for the sake of uses, or goods for the sake of goods, which are done by man in behalf of the church, his country, human society, and a fellow-citizen; for this is loving God and loving the neighbor, since all uses and all goods are from God, and are the neighbor who is to be loved. But he who loves these for the sake of himself loves them merely as servants, because they are serviceable to him; consequently it is the will of one who is in self-love that the church, his country, human societies, and his fellow-citizens, should serve him, and not he them, for he places himself above them and places them beneath himself. Therefore so far as any one is in love of self he separates himself from heaven, because he separates himself from heavenly love. (HH 557)

[A]ll things that have form in the natural world are effects, and all things that have form in the spiritual world are the causes of these effects. There does not take place a natural that does not derive its cause from a spiritual. (DLW 134)

The more one is absorbed in so-called philosophy, the greater is one's delusion and blindness. Delusion and philosophy walk together. There are many cases which provide testimony to this fact. (Commentary on the Book of Isaiah)[65]

I have also been taught by experience, when in the heavens, I was led about hither and thither, which happened when I was awake—that when I lapsed into thoughts concerning worldly things, that which I had perceived in the heavenly mansion instantly disappeared; so that those who let their thoughts down into the world fall down from heaven. (SD 304)

[W]hen, however, I intensely adhered to worldly things in thought, as when I had care concerning necessary expense, about which I this day wrote a letter, so that my mind was for some time detained therewith, I fell, as it were, in a corporeal state, so that the spirits could not converse with me, as they also said, because they were as though absent [from me].

(*SD* 1166)

In the natural world the speech of man is twofold, because his thought is twofold, exterior and interior; for a man can speak from interior thought and at the same time from exterior thought, and he can speak from exterior thought and not from interior, yea, contrary to interior thought, whence come dissimulations, flatteries, and hypocrisies. But in the spiritual world man's speech is not twofold, but single. He there speaks as he thinks, otherwise the sound is harsh and offends the ear; but yet he may be silent, and so not publish the thoughts of his mind. Therefore, a hypocrite, when he comes among the wise, either goes away, or retires to a corner of the room and withdraws himself from observation, and sits silent.   (*AR* 294)

[T]o do good to the neighbor for the sake of God, and thus with God, and from God, is what is called religion.   (*AR* 484)

In a word, love of self and love of the world are altogether contrary to love to the Lord and love towards the neighbour; and therefore love of self and love of the world are infernal loves; indeed, they reign in hell and they also make hell with man. But love to the Lord and love towards the neighbour are heavenly loves; they reign in heaven and also make heaven with man.   (*New Jerusalem and Its Heavenly Doctrine* 78)

There are five sorts who read my works: first, those who reject them from the start, either because they possess completely different beliefs, or because they do not have any beliefs at all. As for the second type, they consider my words to be mere phenomena of the mundane world, reading them only to satisfy their curiosity. A third class reads with discriminating intellect, enjoying them somewhat, but as for truly applying them to life, not a trace of progress can be seen. Those in the fourth class receive with faith, so that their lives are improved to a certain degree, and they make use of them. Those of the fifth sort accept with joy, and are confirmed in their practical lives. (*SD* 2955).[66]

Love is the union of spirits. Love is spiritual fire, spiritual heat. Within people's hearts is the heat of the living spirit, and feeling this is love. The power of love does not go out; it is like heat, like fire.

Love is the life of man; therefore, love makes the man. (The above two passages appear throughout *Conjugial Love*.)[67]

People's humanity lies in their love and will, not in their intellect. Therefore, no matter how great their intellect, if their love is meager, they will be manipulated by love. (This is Swedenborg's principal doctrine; it appears throughout his writings.)[68]

[I]nnocence is the essence of every good, and good is good so far as innocence is within it; and as wisdom is of the life and thence of good, wisdom is wisdom so far as it partakes of innocence. And so with love, charity, and faith. And then it is that no one can enter heaven unless he is in innocence. (*CL* 414)

Notes

1. In the original Japanese, Suzuki wrote, "Second year of Taishô." In Japan, time is divided according to the reigns of emperors; the Taishô emperor's reign lasted from 1912 to 1926. All notes in the translation are supplied by the translator and are not found in Suzuki's original manuscript.

2. Suzuki includes the Chinese character for the word *self* alongside the Latin *proprium*. *Proprium*, meaning "what belongs to oneself," is the word Swedenborg uses for our capacity to experience life

as if we were independent of the One (God). See Michael Stanley, *Emanuel Swedenborg: Essential Readings* (Wellingborough, UK: Aquarian Press: 1988), 27–28.

3. Mencius (Meng Tzu) and Hsün Tzu were Confucian thinkers active in the fourth and third centuries B.C.E. in China.

4. See R.L. Tafel, *Documents concerning the Life and Character of Emanuel Swedenborg,* vol. 2 (London: Swedenborg Society, 1877), 416.

5. In the original Suzuki wrote "Meiji 43." The Meiji period dates from 1868 to 1912.

6. "Opening Session," *Transactions of the International Sweden-borg Congress, Held in Connection with the Celebration of the Swe-denborg Society's Centenary, London, July 4 to 8, 1910* (London: The Swedenborg Society, 1912), 1–2.

7. Swedenborg to Dr. G.A. Beyer, Stockholm, 13 Nov. 1769. See Tafel, vol. 2, doc. 243, pp. 279–280.

8. The thesis is entitled *L. Annaei Senecae et Pub. Syri Mimi . . . Publico examini modeste submittit Emanuel Swedberg, Upsla, 1709* (Select Sentences from Publius Syrus Mimus and L. Annaeus Seneca . . .). For more information, see Cyriel Odhner Sigstedt, *The Swe-denborg Epic: The Life and Works of Emanuel Swedenborg* (New York: Bookman Associates, 1952), 12. Suzuki wrote, "Swedenborg was graduated at the age of 22, receiving a degree in philosophy." However, Sigstedt points out Swedenborg's "graduation" did not involve the granting of a degree in the modern sense.

9. This little-known work is entitled *The Rule of Youth* (1709). In the manuscript it states, "Executed for the most reverend and the most deserving father and bishop, Doctor Jesper Swedberg's, The rule of youth and mirror of old-age."

10. Swedenborg to Eric Benzelius, 21 January 1718. See Tafel, vol. 1, doc. 77, p. 294.

11. The Buddhist term "ultimate truth" (in Japanese, *Daiichigitai;* in Sanskrit, *Paramârtha-satya)* refers to one of two aspects of reality, the other being reality in the conditional or worldly sense (in Japanese, *Sezokutai;* in Sanskrit, *Samvrti-satya).* For a reference work on Japanese Buddhist terminology, see Hisao Inagaki, *A Dictionary of Japanese Buddhist Terms* (Union City, CA: Heian International, 1989).

12. Concerning the latter two works, Suzuki is referring to *Om wattnens högd och förra werldens starcka ebb och flod* (On the

depth of water and strong tides in the primeval world) and *Under-rettelse om docken, slysswercken, och saltwercket* (Information on docks, canal locks, and salt works), both published in 1719. The treatise on copper sheets may be a 1722 treatise entitled *Stormägstigste Allernådigste Konung* (Most mighty and gracious king), a memorandum on an improved process for working copper.

13. This work is titled *Ödmiukast Memorial* (Most humble memorial) and is generally called "The State of Finances in Sweden."

14. *Prodromus philosophia rationcinantis de infinito et causa finali creationis: Deque mechanismo operationis animae et corporis* (The philosophical discourse on the infinite and the final cause of creation; and on the mechanism of the soul and body) (Dresden and Leipzig: Frederick Hekel, 1734).

15. The first treatise mentioned is *Oeconomia regni animalis* (London and Amsterdam, 1740–41), a two-part work. The second work is *Regnum animale*, a treatise in three parts. Parts 1 and 2 were published in The Hague in 1744, the first part concerning the viscera of the abdomen (in Swedenborg's terminology, the "organs of the inferior region"); the second, the viscera of the thorax (the "organs of the superior region"). Part 3 of *Regnum animale*, published in London in 1745, deals with the skin, the senses of touch and taste, and organic forms in general.

16. Where Suzuki simply writes "fibre" *(sen-i)*, Swedenborg wrote, "and their medullary fibre; also the nervous fibre of the body; and the muscular fibre." See *The Animal Kingdom*, trans. James John Garth Wilkinson (London: Swedenborg Society, 1843; rpt. Bryn Athyn, PA: Swedenborg Scientific Association, 1960), 10.

17. *The Animal Kingdom*, 10–11; 12. Swedenborg's final sentence reads, "Thus I hope, that by bending my course inwards continually, I shall open all the doors that lead to her, and at length contemplate the soul herself: by the divine permission."

18. *De cultu et amori Dei* is a three-part work that is unlike any other work by Swedenborg. It is written in the form of a fable or creation drama; however, not all of it was published during Swedenborg's lifetime.

19. The word I've translated as "salvation" is *hongan* in Japanese *(pûrva-prandihâna* in Sanskrit). It means literally "original vow" and typically refers to a vow made by Amida Buddha *(amita* or "infinite" Buddha in Sanskrit) to save all sentient beings. Adherents of

Jôdo ("Pure Land") Buddhism aim for salvation in Amida's Pure Land, a realm where all sentient beings may attain enlightenment. For more information, see n. 46 in the introduction.

20. See R.L. Tafel, *Documents,* "Robsahm's Memoirs of Swedenborg," vol. 1, doc. 5, pp. 35–36. Where Suzuki writes, "Afterwards the Lord daily opened my soul's eyes," Tafel has translated, "Afterwards the Lord opened, daily very often, my bodily *(lekamlig)* eyes."

21. In Japanese, the terms for "self-power" and "other-power" are *jiriki* and *tariki,* respectively. *Tariki* refers to the saving power of a buddha or *bodhisattva,* in particular, to that of Amida Buddha (see note 19, above). Understanding that reliance upon oneself is not sufficient for salvation, believers in *tariki* put their complete faith in Amida's vow to save them.

22. Suzuki mistakenly wrote "1747."

23. Suzuki actually wrote, "Jesus is my best light," but that is not the correct translation of the original Swedish *Jesus är min vän then bäste.* See *Emanuel Swedenborg's Journal of Dreams,* trans. C.T. Odhner (Bryn Athyn, PA: The Academy Bookroom, 1918), 21, sec. 45, April 4–5.

24. Ibid., 24, sec. 45, April 5–6. For the Hebrew term *Zebaoth,* Suzuki has translated "Lord of Hosts."

25. Tafel, vol. 2, pt. 1, doc. 209, p. 172. The *Journal of Dreams* (translated into English after Suzuki produced *Suedenborugu*) contains similar sentiments: "The thought at once occured to me, how great is the grace of the Lord, which accounts to us that we have resisted in temptation, and which is imputed to us, when nevertheless it is nothing but the grace and operation of God, being His and not our own, and He overlooks the weaknesses that we have shown in it. . . ." *(Journal,* 23, sec. 42, April 5–6). And "I ought not to ascribe anything to myself, but that everything is His, although He of grace appropriates the same to us" *(Journal,* 29, sec. 60, April 6–7).

26. I have translated this passage directly from Suzuki's Japanese; he does not provide his source. There is a similar wording in Swedenborg's letter to Thomas Hartley in 1769, known as "Swedenborg's Autobiography: *Responsum ad Epistulam ab Amico ad me Scriptam.*" Here Swedenborg wrote, "My sole object in tendering my resignation was, that I might have more leisure to devote to the new office to which the Lord had called me. A higher post of honour

was then offered me, which I positively declined, lest my heart should be inspired with pride" (Tafel, vol. 1, doc. 2, p. 7). Swedenborg's official letter of resignation to the king can be found in Tafel, vol. 1, doc. 166b, pp. 464–465.

27. Actually, the standard edition of Swedenborg's *Arcana Coelestia* contains twelve volumes. See *Arcana Coelestia,* trans. John Clowes, rvd. John F. Potts (West Chester, PA: The Swedenborg Foundation, [v.d]). Further references to this work will be cited in the text as *AC.*

28. Suzuki wrote "Meiji 43," according to the Japanese system.

29. The "Way" *(Tao)* denotes the ultimate truth in Chinese philosophy.

30. See *Heaven and Its Wonders and Hell: From Things Heard and Seen,* trans. J. C. Ager (West Chester, PA: Swedenborg Foundation, rpt. 1995), v–viii. All subsequent quotations are taken from this edition and will be cited in the text as *HH.* The original Latin title is *De Coelo et Ejus Mirabilibus, et de Inferno.* Suzuki translated this work into Japanese *(Tenkai to Jigoku)* in 1910.

31. Swedenborg assigned paragraph numbers to his works. These numbers are uniform in all editions and are used in Swedenborg studies in place of page numbers.

32. The last sentence seems to be paraphrased from the longer passage in *Heaven and Hell:* "[L]ikewise, what a deed or work is apart from love, namely, that it is not a deed or work of life, but a deed or work of death, which possesses an appearance of life from an evil love and a belief in what is false. This appearance of life is what is called spiritual death."

33. *De Ultimo Judicio, et de Babylonia destructa: ita quod omnia, quae in Apocalypsi praedicta sunt, hodie impleta sint. Ex auditis et visis* (London: 1758). This work contains a uniquely Swedenborgian claim: that the last judgment predicted in the Bible had already taken place in the spiritual world in the year 1757. Swedenborg regarded this judgment as signalling the end of the "old" Christian church, with the second coming of Christ ushering in a new Christianity, culminating with the establishment in the spiritual world of a new Christian church in the year 1770. See G.F. Dole and R.H. Kirven, *A Scientist Explores Spirit* (West Chester, PA: The Swedenborg Foundation, 1992), 75. Later references in the text to this work are taken

from *The Last Judgment*, in *Miscellaneous Theological Works of Emanuel Swedenborg*, trans. John Whitehead, 2nd. edition (New York: Swedenborg Foundation, 1996), and will be referred to in the text as *LJ*.

34. *De Telluribus in Mundo nostro Solari, quae vocantur Planetae: et de telluribus in coelo astrifero: deque illarum incolis; tum de spiritibus et angeli ibi; ex auditis et visis* (London: 1758). This work is often referred to as *Earths in the Universe*.

35. *De Nova Hierosolyma et ejus Doctrina coelesti: ex auditis e coelo. Quibus praemittur aliquid de Nova Coelo et nova Terra* (London: 1758). Suzuki translated this work into Japanese *(Shin Erusaremu to Sono Kyôsetsu)* in 1914.

36. *De Divino Amore et de Divina Sapientia* (Amsterdam: 1763). Suzuki translated this work into Japanese *(Shinchi to Shin'ai)* in 1914. Later references in the text to this work are taken from *Divine Love and Wisdom*, trans. John C. Ager, 2nd edition (West Chester, PA: Swedenborg Foundation, 1995), and will be referred to in the text as *DLW*.

37. The word here translated as "himself" is *jibun* in Japanese, a word that is actually not gender specific. Since the texts used by Suzuki would have assigned the male pronoun to God, that is what is used here.

38. Concerning Swedenborg's breathing techniques, see Sigstedt, *Swedenborg Epic*, pp. 5, 144, 221, and 462, n. 374.

39. The works Suzuki refers to are *Doctrina Novae Hierosolymae de Domino* ("the Lord"), *Doctrina Novae Hierosolymae de Scriptura Sacra* ("Sacred Scripture"), *Doctrina Vitae pro Nova Hierosolyma ex Praeceptis Decalogi* ("Life"), and *Doctrina Novae Hierosolymae de Fide* ("Faith").

40. *Sapientia Angelica de Divina Providentia* (Amsterdam: 1764). Suzuki translated this work into Japanese in 1915 *(Shinryo Ron)*. Later references to this work are taken from *Divine Providence*, trans. William F. Wunsch, 2nd edition (West Chester, PA: Swedenborg Foundation, 1996), and will be referred to in the text as *DP*.

41. In Japanese, the phrase "expedient means" is *hôben* and in Sanskrit, *upâya*.

42. In Swedenborg's use, *proprium*, or an illusion of self-reliance, is not always a negative concept. The term has variant senses, such

as *proprium* that is angelic, diabolical, human, divine, infernal, intellectual, voluntary, etc. In its negative usages, it often means very much the same as pride. From "Glossary of Swedenborgian Terms," *Emanuel Swedenborg: A Continuing Vision,* ed. Robin Larsen, et al (New York: The Swedenborg Foundation, 1988), 515.

43. *Delitiae Sapientiae de Amore Conjugiali; post quas sequuntur voluptates insaniae de Amore scortatorio* (Amsterdam: 1768). Hereinafter references to this work will be cited as *CL.* This work is also entitled *Marital Love,* trans. W. F. Wunsch (New York: Swedenborg Foundation, 1938).

44. *De Commercio Animae et Corporis.* Concerning this work, James Hyde notes, "The book was not 'published' in the general acceptance of the word, but distributed privately. Copies were sent to the various scientific societies and universities of England and France" *(A Bibliography of the Works of Emanuel Swedenborg,* ed. J. Hyde [London: The Swedenborg Society, 1906], 519). This work is also called *Soul-Body Interaction.*

45. Suzuki indicated that the *Spiritual Diary,* also known as the *Memorabilia,* covers "from 1747 to his last year," i.e., 1772. However, Swedenborg stopped writing down his thoughts and experiences in this form in 1765, although in works dated 1766–1771, he included material similar to much of the data in this work, identifying these accounts as "memorable relations" or "memorable occurrences." The first such work to contain these experiences is Swedenborg's *Apocalypse Revealed,* published in 1766. In a letter written to his friend Dr. Gabriel A. Beyer, Swedenborg states:

> I have at last brought the Book of Revelation to a close . . . At the conclusion of every chapter there are memorable relations separated from the text by asterisks which you will please to read first. From these a thorough knowledge may be gathered of the wretched state into which the Reformed Churches have been brought by Faith alone.

See second letter of Swedenborg to Beyer, 8 April 1766 (Tafel, *Documents,* vol. 2, pt. 1, doc. 223, p. 239).

46. The first collected edition in Latin of Swedenborg's spiritual experiences is *Eman. Swedenborgii Diarii Spiritualis,* ed. J.F.I. Tafel,

5 vols. (London: Wm. Newbery, 1843–47). The first complete English translation is *The Spiritual Diary of Emanuel Swedenborg, being the record during twenty years of his supernatural experience*, ed. George Bush, John H. Smithson and James Buss, 5 vols. (London: James Speirs, 1883–1902). Subsequent references to *The Spiritual Diary* will be cited in the text as *SD*.

47. I have translated the Japanese term *innen* as "strong bond" in this sentence, but it could also be translated as the Buddhist term *karma*.

48. This letter was dated "1758" in Borowski's *Life of Kant,* but subsequent scholarship has disputed its date. Tafel originally placed it at 1768 (*Documents*, vol. 2, pt. 1, doc. 272); Signe Toksvig agreed with Tafel (*Emanuel Swedenborg: Scientist and Mystic* [New Haven: Yale University Press, 1948; rpt. New York: Swedenborg Foundation, 1983), 373, n. 14]). However, C.O. Sigstedt has shown that that letter was written in 1763 (*Swedenborg Epic* [New York: Bookman Associates, 1952], 472, n. 567). Likewise, although the German original says the fire took place in September 1756, it actually happened on July 29, 1759. The parenthetical statements that note these discrepancies are Suzuki's own.

49. See Tafel, *Documents,* vol. 2, part 1, doc. 273, 628–629.

50. The portrait was painted for Count von Höpken by P. Krafft, the elder, about the year 1770. In the portrait, Swedenborg holds in his left hand a book inscribed *Apocalypsis Relevata* (sic) *in Qua Deteguntur Arcana Qua ipsi* (sic) *Praedicta Sunt.* The picture appeared as a frontispiece in *Suedenborugu.*

51. Tafel, vol. 2, part 1, doc. 256, p. 445.

52. Ibid., 445–446. In the Japanese, Suzuki omits Cuno's initial expression of surprise. Otherwise, Suzuki's version is close enough to Tafel's English that I have quoted directly from Tafel.

53. The Japanese mistakenly states that von Höpken knew Swedenborg for "forty-five" years.

54. Tafel, vol. 2, part 1, doc. 252a, pp. 407–408.

55. The bracketed paragraph is translated directly from Suzuki but is not found in Tafel immediately following the preceding paragraph. In document 252a, a letter dated May 11, 1772, Count von Höpken writes, "[Swedenborg] was likewise a natural philosopher, but on Cartesian principles. He detested metaphysics, as founded on fallacious ideas, because they transcend our sphere, by means of

which theology has been drawn from its simplicity, and become artificial and corrupted" (Ibid.) In a later letter, dated May 21, 1773, the count writes, "The late Swedenborg certainly was a pattern of sincerity, virtue, and piety, and at the same time, in my opinion, the most learned man in this kingdom" (Tafel, vol. 2, part 1, doc. 252b, p. 410). It appears that Suzuki paraphrased these two sentiments in creating his own paragraph.

56. Tafel, vol. 2, pt. 1, doc. 256a, p. 446.

57. Characteristically, Suzuki did not provide the reference for this quotation.

58. This passage may be a loose translation from *Arcana Coelestia* 1002, which states the following:

> Eating the flesh of animals, regarded in itself, is something profane, for in the most ancient time they never ate the flesh of any beast or bird, but only seeds, especially bread made from wheat, also the fruit of trees, vegetables, various milks and what was made from them, such as various butters. To kill animals and eat their flesh was to them a wickedness, and like wild beasts. They took from them only service and use, as is evident from *Genesis* i. 29, 30. But in the process of time, when men began to be as fierce as wild beasts, and even fiercer, they then for the first time began to kill animals and eat their flesh; and because such was man's nature, it was permitted him to do this, and is still permitted, to this day; and so far as he does it from conscience, so far it is lawful for him, since his conscience is formed of all that he supposes to be true and thus lawful.

59. This passage may be a paraphrase of a quote from Robsahm's memories, as recorded by Tafel: "Those who are poorest are either lazy or good for nothing; and, moreover, alms are often injurious to those that receive them, when any one from mere goodness of heart takes pity on the indigent." Robsahm then continues, "He did not lend money; 'for,' said he, 'this is the direct way to lose it;' moreover, he added, that he had need of all his money for his travels, and for the printing of his works." These latter statements are echoed by Suzuki in the following paragraph. See Tafel, vol. 1, doc. 5, p. 42.

60. Tafel, vol. 2, pt. 2, doc. 305, p. 790. Pernety was a Benedictine monk who became abbot of St. Germain. A catalog of Swedenborg's

writings is included in his French translation of *Heaven and Hell (Les Merveilles du Ciel et de l'Enfer* . . . [Berlin, 1782]).

61. Tafel, vol. 2, part 1, doc. 256f, p. 482.

62. Tafel, vol. 2, part 2, doc. 291, p. 725. This anecdote was related by Fryxell to the secretary of the Swedish Academy, Baron von Beskow. The first few sentences of Tafel's version differ slightly from Suzuki's version: "My grandmother, Sara Greata Askbom, who was married to Anders Ekman, councillor of commerce and burgomaster, had grown up in the neighbourhood of Björngardsgatan in the Södermalm, where her father lived not far from Swedenborg, with whom he had frequent intercourse. The pretty maiden, only fifteen or sixteen years old, had often asked 'Uncle' Swedenborg to show her a spirit or an angel. . . ."

63. *The Spiritual Diary of Emanuel Swedenborg*, trans. George Bush and John H. Smithson (London: James Speirs, 1883), vol. 3, p. 70, para. 3464. There are some slight discrepancies between Suzuki's translation and the Bush/Smithson translation. Where Suzuki says, "I was first accustomed thus to feel my internal breath," *The Spiritual Diary* reads, "I was first accustomed thus to respire. . . ." Where Suzuki writes, "and especially when deeply engaged in writing philosophical works," *The Diary* states, "and especially when deeply engaged in writing the works that have been published." Finally, where Suzuki writes, "I was thus from the period of childhood able to stop my external breathing and activate only my internal breath," *The Diary* states, "I was thus during many years, from the period of childhood, introduced into such respirations . . . ."

64. CL 239–242.

65. Emanuel Swedenborg, *A New Translation from the Hebrew of the Prophet Isaiah* . . . , trans. J. H. Smithson (London: Longman, Green, Longman, and Roberts, 1860). Suzuki did not supply the paragraph number for this citation. However, Swedenborg expressed similar sentiments in his *Spiritual Diary,* vol. 1, 767 and vol. 2, 2263.

66. This entry is dated August 27, 1748. Suzuki's version differs enough from that of Bush and Smithson that the above text is translated directly from the Japanese. Bush and Smithson's translation reads as follows:

> I spoke with spirits (as to) how my writings concerning these things seem to be received when they become public; for evil

spirits sometimes infused that no one would perceive these things, but that (men) would reject them. Now while in the street and talking with spirits, it was given to perceive that there are five kinds of reception: First, (those) who wholly reject, who are in another persuasion, and who are enemies of the faith. These reject; for it cannot be received by them, since it (can) not penetrate their minds. Another class, who receive these things as scientifics, and are delighted with them as scientifics, and as curious things. A third class, which receives, intellectually, so that they receive with sufficient alacrity, but still remain (in respect to) life as before. A fourth class (receives) persuasively, so that it penetrates to the improvement of their lives; they recur to these in certain states, and make use of them. A fifth class, who receive with joy, and are confirmed.

67. For example, see *CL* 183(3), 269(2), 361, and 380(6). The parenthetical remark is Suzuki's.

68. For example, see *AC* 33 and 10130(2); *HH* 479 and 481(2). The parenthetical remark is Suzuki's.

*Swedenborg's View of Heaven
and "Other-Power"*

**A Translation of "Suedenborugu:
Sono Tenkai to Tarikikan"**

D. T. Suzuki, 1963

Swedenborg's View of Heaven and "Other-Power"

Swedenborg's religious philosophy is unfathomably deep; and since it is fairly difficult to grasp, few people have made a scholarly study of it. However, when you carefully read his seemingly absurd writing with a calm mind, you find that many elements become rather difficult to dismiss. In particular, Swedenborg's *Heaven and Hell* contains profound and fascinating points. Among his many works, this is the one most widely read; and having formerly translated it into Japanese, I would like to take the opportunity to express my feelings on it, although this essay is really no more than an introduction.

Swedenborg does not give a very clear definition of heaven. It might be considered a state after death, or it might be that this world, just as it is, is heaven—or hell, depending on how you take it. In truth, even among the spirits dwelling in heaven, there are very few who can see what heaven is. Because of this, it may be impossible to explain to ordinary people like us.

Be that as it may, we can see heaven as a kind of ideal realm with a relationship to the material world of the five senses that is one of neither equivalence nor separation. Swedenborg uses the word "state" to describe it.

Heaven comprises the good of love and the truth of enlightenment. When good and truth return to a state of innocence, they reveal a perfect heaven. Unless one enters a state of "no false thoughts" or "artlessness,"[1] even good is not divine good and truth is not divine truth. One aspect of this condition is reflected in the speech and actions of children. However, the innocent nature of children is unrefined, so it cannot be called the genuine state.

As for the source of innocence, it spontaneously floods the inner life when we completely give up our own thoughts. Doing good, we do not think it good. When others comment on it and call it good, that good is not something that arises from the self but arises from the Divine. Nothing results from self-power; everything is achieved through the addition of divine power to oneself: "Those who are in a state of innocence attribute nothing of good to themselves, but regard all things as received and ascribe them to the Lord . . . and wish to be led by Him and not by themselves. . . ."[2] All of the highest angels dwell in the purity of this innocence. When the degree of purity is low, the angel's position in heaven naturally falls as well. The quality of innocence is actually the fundamental principle on which heaven's organization is based.

Because heaven derives from innocence, the fact that the Divine in heaven is also innocent is a self-evident truth. Swedenborg occasionally spoke with angels and related what transpired. Innocence is the essence of every good and good is truly good to the extent that it has innocence within it. What we call wisdom is wisdom only when it arises from this innocence, and the same holds true for love, charity, and faith. Therefore, when they are not innocent, people cannot enter heaven. The Lord expressed this meaning in the following verse: "Let the children come to me; do not try to stop them; for the kingdom of heaven belongs to such as these. I tell you, whoever does not accept the kingdom of God like a child will never enter it" [Mark 10:14; Luke 18:16]. The children spoken of here signify innocence. According to Swedenborg, the

Bible is composed of many of these symbols. Having become conscious of their hidden meanings, he wrote a number of different works. This awareness is not something that came from his own mind. He personally entered heaven and experienced it as it flowed from God.

Swedenborg's symbolic philosophy is built on the principle of correspondence. Because this principle is one of the major tenets of his philosophy, one certainly must know about it to understand Swedenborg. I believe the principle of correspondence originally comes from the idea in the Bible that "God created man in his own image" [Genesis 1:27].

Those without the perfect good of love and the perfect truth of wisdom cannot understand the hidden will of heaven. People have both an internal and an external; and not being able to make an adequate correspondence between them, they cannot comprehend [heaven's will]. One way to grasp it, however, is through the phenomena of the sensual world as perceived through the five senses. All of these phenomena contain significance. The caw of a crow or the song of a sparrow are not simply a caw and a song: there are heavenly significance and infernal significance. This kind of reading depends on the principle of correspondence. Therefore, while people are on the earth, they are free to unveil their correspondence with heaven according to the nature of their internal enthusiasm. That is, this world of suffering can also be considered a Pure Land of tranquil light.[3] Those who grasp the principle of correspondence stroll through a kingdom of significance.

Heaven, in fact, is composed solely of this significance; it is a place governed by pure love and pure truth. Love is warmth and corresponds to the human heart. Truth is light and corresponds to the human lungs. Located in the thorax, the heart and lungs are distinguished from other organs. When love stirs, the heart throbs and heat is released. When truth shines, the breath is regulated and there is silence. However, when there is no heat, there is no light, so light is of secondary importance. Even without light, there is heat, heat being the fundamental principle. Dark heat is the fire of hell, and it is from here that all pain is born. Heat with light brings spring to the universe, and it always feels like spring in heaven.[4] Here we see the truth of correspondence.

The perfect union of love and wisdom is the individual person, and all of heaven exhibits itself through the appearance of an individual. The full realization of a person's integrity can be seen only in the realm of divine good and divine truth. Among modern philosophers, there are those who say things such as, "God is a perfect individual. Human consciousness, try as it might, can never seize the singularity of the individual. Yet it always tries to grasp it, and this longing is first satisfied upon arrival at the Divine. The reason for the existence of this longing is simply that the Divine realizes itself in individual human beings." Can we not see traces of Swedenborg in this?

The doctrine of correspondence is profound. In terms of Buddhism, it is similar to the Shingon philosophy of phenomena.[5] One can also interpret the idea of the Pure Land according to the doctrine of correspondence. Even if we say that all phenomena interpenetrate without obstacle, we cannot identify hell with paradise.[6] Although we can say that the Pure Land's significance is found in this world of suffering, hell, being hell, is not paradise; and Kannon, Amida, Fudô, Yakushi, and the eight million gods exist just the same.[7] The principle of correspondence cannot be divorced from human consciousness. Viewed from the doctrine of correspondence, I believe Shingon teachings on such things as *mudrâs* can be interpreted in an interesting fashion.[8] If Swedenborg had not communicated with the Christian heaven, and had instead mastered Buddhist philosophy, what kind of "hidden will" would he have discovered? I believe it is worth engaging in this kind of speculation.

Previously, I noted that the essence of heaven is innocence and that, because this innocence cannot be achieved through ordinary knowledge, it must be reached through a perfect enlightenment beyond knowledge. What I call enlightenment is the perception that we cannot independently achieve good separate from the Lord God in heaven. Without this perception, we cannot attain innocence.

Since heaven derives from innocence, its opposite, hell, would have to signify non-innocence. In other words, those who believe in self-power without relying on other-power will always fall into hell.[9] When my ego's purpose suddenly arises, I shoot into hell like an arrow. The purpose of the ego, according to Swedenborg, is self-love and worldly love. When the vault of hell is opened, the raging fire and smoke that one sees rising up is what springs from the blaze of these two loves. Those who are in hell in bodily form are completely consumed by these flames. As I said before, there is also heat in heaven, the heat of divine love. However, this heat is like the warmth of spring, and once this warmth flows into the blaze of hell, the blaze cools and becomes extremely cold. The heat of heaven acts in this mysterious way. Flowing from the depths of the Divine is a power that cannot be judged by human perception.

Swedenborg was allowed by the Lord to witness hell. A portion of his record reads:

> The hells are everywhere, and their entrances, when looked into, appear pitch black. But those who dwell in them think it to be bright. This is because their eyes are adapted to this degree of light. The cave openings first extend inward, and then twist obliquely. Some plunge downward into a bottomless abyss, and appear like the caves of wild beasts. Other hells seem like the ruins of houses and cities after conflagrations.

The spirits living here are engaged in unceasing quarrels, enmities, fightings, and brutalities. Throughout the scorched city, bands of thieves and robbers swagger about. In some of the hells there are nothing but brothels, filled with every kind of filth and excrement. Again, there are thick forests in which spirits roam like wild beasts, and where, underground, there are dens into which those flee who are pursued by others. Some are wastelands where there is only sand. There are those who flee as far as such places. In particular, those who contrived intrigues and deceits while in the world are driven into the desert, where they must spend their lives.[10]

I believe there is no one who has written as minutely about the nature of heaven and hell as Swedenborg. Dante skillfully applied his art, and he should be recognized as an exponent of medieval beliefs; but Swedenborg, with an intellectual faculty forged through science and with his amazing power of imagination and insight, exhaustively described the spiritual world. At first his writing seems ridiculous, but as you read on, you are drawn into it. Although it might contain a number of fantasies, it undoubtedly includes many truths as well.

Swedenborg said that heaven arises from love toward the Lord and knowledge of the Divine. Hell, conversely, is realized through love of self and love of the world, as well as through consciousness of both these loves. Heaven and hell are opposite poles. Recognizing these poles, Swedenborg made human beings the mid-point. Self-love means grabbing pleasure from others and gathering it only to yourself. Worldly love is the desire to make another person's possessions your own. Those in the midst of this sort of love may wish to share their own enjoyment with others; but since the focus of that motive is still themselves, they do not increase the enjoyment of others, but instead reduce it. Swedenborg said he personally experienced this in the spiritual world. Before Swedenborg applied himself to religion, he was a prominent scientist, so he did not give abstract explanations. He taught through his own observations. Thus, in the spiritual world, he sensed that when an egotist merely approached a heavenly society, the level of enjoyment among the angels in that society would decline. Swedenborg said the degree of this decline was proportional to the intensity of self-love felt by infernal beings. He never explained by way of argument or speculation, but with the attitude of a scientist describing actual experiences. In this respect, he had a unique worldview.

Heaven is divine love, and hell is self-love, while we, in between, must decide our lot for ourselves. Swedenborg called this freedom equilibrium. I find it interesting how his choice of the word "equilibrium" demonstrates that he was a scientist. In any case, we are free and may head toward the love of heaven or love of hell as we please. Without free and independent action, true regeneration and salvation are not possible. Without freedom, we cannot act according to our own love. Love that flows from the internal originates with the Lord; but when we do not act from this love, we never attain our true life. Because the external comes from memory, it works only through thought, and conceptual living cannot save people. In all cases, it is necessary to express the internal will, for it is in this that correspondence with heaven may take place.

According to Swedenborg's description, there are two gates that people open. One leads to hell and the other to heaven. Evil and falsehood flow from one direction, and good and truth from the other. Evil people open wide the gate to hell and wantonly accept its flow. As for the gate to heaven, several rays of light barely thrust through a crack above. The fact that evil people also possess the faculties of thought, philosophical reasoning, and linguistic expression is due to the power of this light. However, they do not recognize that these [faculties] are from heaven, thinking them only to be [the properties] of their own reasonable minds. Because of this, the true nature of these reasonable minds is love for the infernal. All of their thoughts are stained by this love and are in darkness. However, they imagine they are in the light. Swedenborg entered into and observed the interior of these sorts of people. Standing at the entrance to the gate of hell, they smell the foul stench that spills out—a stench that induces nausea and dizziness—and laughing merrily, take pleasure in it. If, by any chance, they feel the breath of heaven, these people cannot endure the internal suffering, and with one loud voice cry, "What pain!"

From the viewpoint of human beings, this is a manifestation of free nature; but the divine will, which has granted to humans the sensation of freedom, tries, based on this freedom, to build the salvation of people through their volition. In truth, the desire of people to go to heaven is an act of the divine will, or other-power. Again, to have this intention, to be reborn in heaven, is impossible without the other-power of the divine will; but from the perspective of freedom, everything seems to be the result of the self-power of human beings. The reason that people must perceive the reasoning of an autonomous will is that, if they do not, they will not be able to think about and intend evil and falsehood. A thinking consciousness is a condition for this freedom, which allows for the manifestation of an internal that tends toward good and truth. Despite the teaching of salvation through other-power, if we first do not recognize the consequences of *karma* and the depth of our evil passions,[11] other-power can do nothing to help. The possibility of listening stems from free consciousness.

Through the freedom and reason that are granted by other-power, a Buddhist recognizes his or her sins and achieves rebirth in paradise, while a Christian gains repentance and resurrection. The need to repent comes from the fact that we are originally in a state of degeneration. Our life is nourished by the heat and light of heaven on the one hand, but fueled by self-love and worldly love on the other. Through these two loves, divine good and divine wisdom are suppressed; stopped by various falsehoods and evils, we forget to advance. We are awakened from this by the words of the Bible, or in Buddhism, by the name of Amida, the name that sounds throughout the ten directions. When freedom and reason are not guided by infernal love, but instead turn toward the sun in heaven—that is, the chief direction of the Divine—the love and light of the Divine flood that person's interior to the point of overflowing, and in this is the reality of regeneration. This regeneration is accompanied by a heavenly joy. At first, we think this joy is something natural and do not recognize its origin in the Divine; but the moment of recognition finally comes, and this moment is perfect enlightenment. We realize that various goods and truths stem from the other-power of the Divine and that the consciousness of autonomous self-power comes from a blind thought, marked with traces of self-love. Without the truth of this enlightenment, there is no real regeneration. The perfect union of this truth with divine love allows us to lead a spiritual life. This is said to be the moment when we live the life of the internal.

Evil people too are able to discern through reason what is good. Yet, because that good has not entered into their lives, their interiors are not illuminated by the light of regeneration, and they turn their backs to the Divine. Because Swedenborg witnessed this in the spiritual world, it must be true. Imagine here a conversation between two people. It appears very intimate, and when you listen to them, it feels as if you can discern their internal love. However, viewed with Swedenborg's insight, these two people are standing back to back, and the waves of love arising from their inner hearts are dark in color. It looks as if they are crashing into each other. The internal and external of this world are separated in this way, so that the activity of spiritual reason is not clear. But when we enter the world of the internal, everything is unconcealed and naked. The Bible says, "For there is nothing hidden that will not become public, nothing under cover that will not be made known" [Luke 8:17]. When we recall this, everything is a self-evident truth, says Swedenborg. This is again the force of other-power.

There is a great deal I wish to write concerning Swedenborg, but that remains for another day. He was a Swede who died in England in 1772, that is, 155 years ago. He was a man of science until age 55, and his works on theology, more than most could write in a lifetime, span the next [twenty-nine] years. When he was 84 years old, he predicted the time of his death and accordingly returned to heaven.

Notes

1. In Japanese, *shija-nashi* and *mukôyô*. The quotation marks appear in Suzuki's text.

2. Emanuel Swedenborg, *Heaven and Its Wonders and Hell*, 2nd ed., trans. John C. Ager (West Chester, PA: The Swedenborg Foundation, 1995), 277. As is standard in Swedenborgian studies, the number refers to a paragraph, not a page.

3. In Japanese, "this world of suffering" is *shaba* and in Sanskrit, *sahâ*. This is the mundane world in which people endure various forms of pain. In Japanese, *jakkôjôdo* is a standard designation for a Buddhist Pure Land. In the context of this essay, Suzuki is referring to the Pure Land of Amida Buddha. See my introduction, n. 46, p. xxxiii.

4. The phrase translated here as "universe" is *sanzendaisensekai* in Japanese and *trisâhasra-mahâsâhasrâḥ lokadhâtavaḥ* in Sanskrit. The term means literally "triple-thousand great one-thousand world." A thousand worlds make a small one-thousand world *(shôsen-sekai)*; a thousand of these make a medium one-thousand world *(chûsen-sekai)*; a thousand of these make a great one-thou-sand world *(daisen-sekai)*. See Hisao Inagaki, *A Dictionary of*

Japanese Buddhist Terms (Union City, CA: Heian International, 1989), 277.

5. Shingon is a school of esoteric Buddhism founded in Japan by Kûkai (774–835). Within the history of Shingon, there have been different ideas and practices surrounding the term *jisô* ("phenomena"); it is not clear to exactly what Suzuki is referring. But, in general, Shingon practitioners maintain that the phenomena of the tangible world are aspects of Mahâvairocana Buddha's continual preaching. Kûkai equated Mahâvairocana (in Japanese, *Dainichi Buddha*) with the Dharmakâya (in Japanese, *hosshin*), which is the "dharma-body" or Buddha body of ultimate reality. In doing so, Kûkai transformed the ultimate body of the Buddha from something formless and beyond conceptualization into a dynamic force approachable through the particular and concrete. Because the Dharmakâya reveals itself through "all objects of sense and thought," one can learn this language and attain enlightment "in this very existence," as Kûkai put it. See Yoshito S. Hakeda, "Essentials of Kûkai's Esoteric Buddhist Thought and Practice," in *Kûkai: Major Works, Translated with an Account of His Life and a Study of His Thought* (New York: Columbia University Press, 1972), 76–100. See also Taiko Yamasaki, *Shingon: Japanese Esoteric Buddhism* (Boston, MA: Shambhala, 1988).

6. The term "interpenetrate" is taken from the Japanese *jijimuge*. This concept, encapsulated by the simple phrase "the one in the many and the many in the one," is attributed primarily to the Hua-Yen school of Buddhist philosophy (in Japanese, the "Kegon" school), but it has also been embraced by other Buddhist schools. In Thomas Cleary's words, it means that "each and every phenomenon implies and reflects the existence of each and every other thing; the existence of all is inherent in the existence of one" *(Entry into the Inconceivable: An Introduction to Hua-Yen Buddhism* [Honolulu, HI: University of Hawaii Press, 1983], 33).

7. Regarding Amida, see my introduction, n. 46. Kannon (in Sanskrit, *Avalokiteśvara*) is a *bodhisattva* who takes on numerous forms, both male and female, and is commonly depicted as an attendant of Amida. Fudô (in Sanskrit, *Acala*) is a fierce spirit who is often depicted holding a sword in his right hand and a rope in his left. He is one of the myôô (in Sanskrit, *vidyâ-râja*), divinities who

protect Buddhists and the Buddhist Dharma. Yakushi, whose full name is *Yakushi-rurikô* (in Sanskrit, *Bhaisajya-guru-vaidûrya-prabha*) is known as the "Medicine Buddha" because one of the twelve vows he made as a *bodhisattva* was to cure disease.

8. *Mudrâs* (in Japanese, *ingei*) are ritual hand gestures associated with certain Buddhas and *bodhisattvas*. Shingon practitioners often form these gestures during meditation.

9. In Japanese, "other-power" is *tariki,* the saving power of the Buddha.

10. This passage seems to be a paraphrase from *Heaven and Hell,* paragraphs 584 and 586.

11. In Japanese, *bonnô;* in Sanskrit, *kleśa.*

The Dharma of Emanuel Swedenborg: A Buddhist Perspective

by David Loy

In January 1887 a former Swedenborgian minister named Carl Herman Vetterling, who now called himself Philangi Dasa, began publishing the first Buddhist journal in the United States. The inaugural issue of *The Buddhist Ray,* which he edited from his cabin in the mountains above Santa Cruz, California, proclaimed itself "devoted to Buddhism in general, and to the Buddhism in Swedenborg in particular." The prospectus on the first page informed readers that it would "set forth the teachings imparted by the Mongolian Buddhists to Emanuel Swedenborg, and published by him in his mystic writings." As this declaration suggests, Philangi Dasa was not afraid of controversy; and whatever the scholarly shortcomings of his journal, it was not dull. "Delivering his unorthodox views with self-righteous conviction, he offended readers regularly, but his outspoken brand of sincerity made *The Buddhist Ray* one of the liveliest Buddhist journals ever."[1]

In the same year Philangi Dasa also published *Swedenborg the Buddhist, or The Higher Swedenborgianism, Its Secrets and Thibetan Origin.* George Dole has tactfully described it as "rather strange,"[2] yet the book is not without its charm. Presented as a 322-page dream, it takes the form of a conversation among Swedenborg himself, a Buddhist monk, a Brahmin, a Parsi, a Chinese, an Aztec, an Icelander, and "a woman." The result is an amiable theosophical synthesis of religious beliefs and mythologies from many lands. As one would expect from his background and the texts available in his time, Philangi Dasa knew more about Swedenborg than about Buddhism; and his ostensible aim, to show that Swedenborg was really a Buddhist, is shadowed by another concern, using Buddhism to reveal the shortcomings of Swedenborgianism. The tone is that of a disappointed lover:

> Although I set much by Swedenborg, I would as soon put a razor in the hands of an infant as to put his theological writings into the hands of a man not versed in the spiritual teachings of Asia in general, and in the teachings of Buddhism in particular; for, he might embrace them and, with a large number of members of the "New Church" society, die in doubt and despair.[3]

Philangi Dasa's journal and book have long been forgotten, yet he was not the only one to notice the similarities between Swedenborg and Buddhism. A few years later D. T. Suzuki was introduced to Swedenborg sometime during his years working with Paul Carus in Illinois (1897–1908).[4] As Andrew Bernstein has explained in his introduction to this volume, Suzuki's interest in Swedenborg was particularly intense over a five-year period (from 1910 to 1915) when he translated into Japanese four of Swedenborg's works and wrote a biography and overview of the Swedish seer's career. Then, in 1924 Suzuki published a nine-page article suggesting that Swedenborg's doctrine of correspondences may be compared with the Shingon doctrine that phenomena are aspects of Mahâvairocana Buddha's ceaseless teaching. The last paragraph concludes: "There is still a great deal I wish to write about Swedenborg, but that remains for another day." Unfortunately,

that day never came: Suzuki's writings on Swedenborg ceased
after this article, although he continued writing for another
fifty years, the majority of his books (totaling perhaps 20,000
pages) being written after his mid-fifties.

Curiously, these later Buddhist writings contain very few al-
lusions to Swedenborg, despite the fact that there are references to, and sometimes detailed discussions of, many other
Western writers, including Christian mystics such as Eckhart.
It is not clear why Swedenborg figures so little in these many
works, although evidently it was not due to any disaffection:
all of Suzuki's published references to Swedenborg are positive, and he was fond of mentioning Swedenborg in conversation. According to his private secretary Mihoko Bekku, as late
as the 1950's, he would sometimes remark, in response to an
inquiry, "Well, Swedenborg would say . . . "[5] And when we
consider the direction that Suzuki's life took after his encounter with Swedenborg, doesn't it suggest that the latter's
personal example—Swedenborg's singleminded yet humble
devotion to the task of recording his spiritual insights—may
have served as an important model for Suzuki?

However influential Suzuki's translations may have been for
the development of Japanese Swedenborgianism, his contribution to the dialogue between Buddhism and Swedenborg
seems, like Dasa's, to have been forgotten. Nevertheless, their
insight was not misplaced, for there indeed are profound similarities between what Swedenborg writes and what Buddhism
teaches; and today we have reached a point where we can ap-
preciate them more fully. In recent years the dialogue between
Buddhism and Christianity has become an important development in contemporary religious thought, yet as far as I know
this dialogue has overlooked Swedenborg. The purpose of this
afterword is to note some of the more important parallels between Swedenborg and Buddhism and to reflect on their

meaning for us. These similarities are all the more interesting because reliable Buddhist teachings and texts were not available in Europe during his time.⁶

Swedenborg's views will be presented by focusing mainly on *Heaven and Hell,* his best-known work, which is also the best summary of his voluminous writings. Since I want to refer to more than one Buddhist tradition, my Buddhist citations will be more eclectic.

The Concept of the Self

The first similarity to be discussed is also the most basic one. *Heaven and Hell* presents a vision of human and postmortem existence that contrasts sharply with our postmodernist suspicion of grand narratives that propose to explain everything. No narrative is or could be grander than Swedenborg's. Yet, like Buddhism with its doctrine of *anâtman* (Sanskrit, "no self"), his vision is postmodern insofar as it denies an ontological self.

In our century psychoanalytic and deconstructive ways of thinking have provided us with some homegrown handles to grasp what remains a very counter-intuitive concept: the notion that our sense-of-self is not self-evident or self-present but a mental construction. Swedenborg agrees with Buddhism that the self (his Latin term is *proprium,* literally "what belongs to oneself," for him the understanding that one thinks and wills from oneself) is an illusion. According to both, the sense-of-self—the sense that I am a self-existing being whose thoughts and actions are self-generated—is better understood as the effect of an economy of forces. For Swedenborg these forces are spiritual—that is, spirits. Good spirits (angels) and bad spirits (demons) are always with us, and their influence accounts for much of what we understand as our mental and emotional life. The evil spirits take up residence in our evil affections and bond there, as do the good spirits in our good affections (*HH* 295).[7] It is because their influence harmonizes with our own affections and tendencies that it enters our way of thinking and is accepted. In this way harmful spirits reinforce our bad character traits, and good spirits our better character traits. Some spirits are the source of our anxiety and depression (*HH* 299). Even diseases (including the toothache that bothered Swedenborg!) and death can be caused by infernal spirits. Each of us has free will—that is, our ability to choose is preserved—because we are balanced between these two complexes of positive and negative spiritual forces.

The natural Buddhist parallel to such an economy of forces is the five *skandha*, "heaps" or aggregates, whose interaction creates the illusion of self, according to the Pali Sutras. However, this particular similarity may or may not be very deep, for within the Buddhist tradition (which, we must remember, originates in oral teachings over 2400 years old, creating textual quagmires that Swedenborgians do not need to worry about) it is not altogether clear what each *skandha* refers to (*rûpa, vedanâ, samjñâ, samskâra,* and *vijñâna* may be translated in various ways) or how their interaction is to be understood (they are usually taken ontologically, but they may refer to five different stages in the cognition of something). Therefore, it is unclear how "spiritual" each *skandha* is, although the earliest Pali commentaries seem to understand them more impersonally and mechanically as processes that lack a self *doing* them.

What remains important, however, is how both deconstructions-of-self challenge the religious and philosophical climates of their own time by denying the existence of a Cartesian-type soul defined by its self-consciousness, which is to be liberated so it can become *pure* consciousness. Just as Buddhism contradicts the Hindu notion of a pure soul or consciousness covered with karmic impurities, so Swedenborg contradicts the Western tradition (going back at least as far as Plato) of a sinful or confused *psyche* that needs to be cleansed so it can shine forth in its uncorrupted glory. Instead, each individual *is* one's inmost affection or ruling love (*HH* 58). In place of such a pristine self-consciousness, Swedenborg emphasizes that what I *love* is what I *am*. What we do, motivated by such love, seems free to us. The religious task is not to discover what resides behind this love—some pure consciousness that is supposedly *doing* the loving—but to transform myself by changing my ruling love (from love of self to love of God and neighbor).

Perhaps this understanding of our mental life becomes more meaningful if we relate Swedenborg's doctrine to two fundamental Mahâyâna Buddhist teachings: the denial of a duality between subject and object and the denial of duality between mind and body. Both resonant deeply with important Swedenborgian claims.

The denial of subject-object nonduality is found in many Mahâyâna canonical texts and commentaries. As the Japanese Zen master Dôgen put it, "I came to realize that mind is no other than mountains and rivers and the great wide earth, the sun and the moon and the stars."[8] If there is no self inside, it also makes no sense to talk about the world as being "outside" one's mind. Everything becomes "my" mind. I think this illuminates a Swedenborgian claim that is otherwise difficult to understand: Swedenborg writes that the divine influx is not experienced as coming *from* our internals; rather it comes through the forehead *into* our internals: "The influx of the Lord Himself into man is into his forehead, and from there into the whole face" (*HH* 251).[9] If I understand this correctly, the implication is a very Buddhist one: not that we must realize the God within (as in so much Christian mysticism), but that the sense of a *within* apart from the world is the self-delusion that needs to be ovecome.

How is this delusion of self to be overcome? Dôgen also
provides a succinct explanation of the Buddhist approach:

> To study the buddha way is to study the self. To study the self
> is to forget the self. To forget the self is to be actualized by
> myriad things. When actualized by myriad things, your body
> and mind as well as the bodies and minds of others drop away.
> No trace of realization remains, and this no-trace continues
> endlessly.[10]

Since there has never been a self, only the illusion of self, the
point of the Buddhist path is not to eliminate the self but to
forget oneself, which is accomplished by becoming so absorbed into one's meditation-exercise that one *becomes* it.
When my sense-of-the-self evaporates, I realize that I *am* the
world. Instead of attaining immortality, I realize that I cannot
die because I was never born.

And how is delusion of self overcome according to Swedenborg? The *Spiritual Diary,* in which he first described his own
experiences in the afterworld, records several conversations
with spirits who did not understand that "we are to undergo
a process of annihilation, or becoming nothing," to which
Swedenborg replied that "this was what I desired, to wit, to be
absolutely nothing, for then I should first begin to be something":

> They were afterwards instructed that by nothing was meant that
> a man should lose all that was his own, that is, his cupidities,
> and so his iniquities, . . . and that they could never be anything
> until they had lost that which was theirs, and that in proportion
> as they experienced that loss, or were reduced to nothing, they
> would begin to be something, and that then they would have
> whatever they desired or thought. . . . (*SD* 2043–4)[11]

For Swedenborg as much as for Buddhism, the path is letting-
go of one's self.

By transforming observed *objects* into *manifestations* of
nondual mind, not only the so-called material world but the

events of "my" mental activity become more "animated," that is, they gain more of a life of their own, independent of being thought by *me*. Swedenborg says something very similar:

> [T]hose things of wisdom and love which are called thoughts, perceptions, and affections, are substances and forms. . . The affections, perceptions and thoughts there [in the brain] are not exhalations but are all actually and really subjects, which do not emit anything from themselves, but merely undergo changes according to whatever flows against and affects them.
> (*DLW* 42)[12]

Then perceptions, thoughts, and feelings are not what "I" do; it is more accurate to turn that around and say that my sense of self is a function of what *they* do. In this way Swedenborg's understanding of our mental life accords with his understanding of how influx operates, both that from the Lord (usually, mediately through angels) and that from evil spirits.

This nonduality of subject and object also has profound consequences for our experience of mind-body duality. So much of twentieth-century philosophy has been concerned with deconstructing dualisms such as mind-body and mind-matter, which are now seen as problematical and alienating, that it is necessary to remember Swedenborg was writing in the eighteenth century when it was less clear that there was any problem or what alternatives there might be. Swedenborg's view of their relation is, therefore, all-the-more striking. In the afterworld, the body of every spirit is the outer form of that spirit's love, corresponding exactly to the inner form of his soul or mind (e.g., *HH* 363). From a person's face, in particular, all the more inward affections are visible and radiate, because faces are the very outward form of these affections (*HH* 47). From conversation, too, the wiser angels know the whole condition of another person (*HH* 236). After death, angels carefully examine one's body, beginning with the face, then the fingers, and so on, because the details of one's thought and intention are written on the entire body as well (*HH* 463). The new spirit is later "devastated" because the outward and inward elements must correspond and act as one (*HH* 498, 503). The result is that the mind and body of a spirit come to correspond so completely that it is no longer meaningful to distinguish between them. This is the basis of that complete conjugial union experienced most fully in the afterworld and sometimes even in this life, for both soul and mind, although they appear to be in the head, are "actually in the whole body" (*CL* 178).[13]

The fact that such union can occur in this world as well reminds us not to draw too sharp a line between the world to come and this one. Bioenergetic therapies such as rolfing confirm that the body is not just a vehicle for mind, for it retains memories of past traumas that can be stimulated by massage.

The Love of the Self

The love of self, which closes our inmost parts to the divine influx (*HH* 272), is the problem to be overcome. With the support of his rationality, man has corrupted the output of the spiritual world within himself "through a disorderly life. So he must be born into complete ignorance and be led back from there into the pattern of heaven by divine means" (*HH* 108).

The need to become ignorant suggests a Buddhist-like critique of conceptualization, which Swedenborg also makes: insights, being outward truths, do not by themselves save us, but the way those insights change us (*HH* 517). Innocence is the *esse* of everything good, and everything is good to the extent it contains innocence (*HH* 281). To a Buddhist this sounds like *tathatâ*, the "just *this!*"-ness that describes the unselfconscious way an enlightened person lives. Having given up the love of self, and let go of the sense of self, we do not attain some other reality but realize the true nature of this one, which is all we need. That is why the essence of Zen can be "chopping wood and carrying water."

The importance of this can hardly be overemphasized because this is how both traditions solve the problem of life. To be spiritual is nothing more than being open to, and thereby united with, the whole: that is, to accept one's position and therefrom manifest the whole, in contrast to self-love (Swedenborg) and the delusion of separate self (Buddhism). The essential point is that this is not something that can happen only after we die. We are in heaven right now if our internals are open, according to Swedenborg, and *nirvâṇa* is to be attained here and now, according to Śâkyamuni Buddha. In fact, *nirvâṇa* is nothing other than the true nature of *saṁsâra*, according to the Mahâyâna tradition. One version of this is that the passions, just as they are, are wisdom and enlightenment. This contradicts the more orthodox view of earlier Pali Buddhism, which understands desire as the source of our *duḥkha* (suffering, dissatisfaction); but the Mahâyâna point is that our desires can be transmuted from selfish cravings into self-less joys. Swedenborg's attitude towards the pleasures of life makes the same critique of earlier ascetic, life-denying versions of Christianity:

> It is by no means forbidden any one to enjoy the pleasures of the body and of sensual things; . . . for these are outermost or corporeal affections from interior affection. The interior affections, which are living, all derive their delight from good and truth; and good and truth derive their delight from charity and faith, and then from the Lord, thus from Life itself; and therefore the affections and pleasures which are from thence are alive. (*AC* 995)[14]

This does not imply that the spiritual life is an epicurean-like devotion to "higher" pleasures, for there is another aspect of *tathatâ*-activity that Swedenborg and Buddhism both emphasize: that, as Swedenborg puts it, the Lord's kingdom is a kingdom of "uses which are ends,"—that is, purposes that are functions; divine worship is not a matter of attending church but living a life of love, charity, and faith (*HH* 112, 221). "People who like to do good for others, not for their own sakes but for the sake of good, are the ones who love the neighbor; for good *is* the neighbor" (*HH* 64). Compare to this a Buddhist proverb that in the beginning one does good deeds for the sake of the neighbor; later (when one has realized that the neighbor too has no self) one does good for the sake of the Dharma (the "Higher Law" of the nature of things as taught by Buddhism); but finally one does good for no reason at all, which in Swedenborg's terms is to attain the highest innocence. For Buddhism such a life is best exemplified by the *bodhisattva*, who, being un-self-preoccupied, is devoted to the endless work of universal salvation. A *bodhisattva* is so unselfconscious that when he or she gives something to someone, it is without the awareness that one is giving, that there is someone else who receives, or even that there is a gift that is given. Such generosity is emphasized as the first and most important (because it is said to include all the others) of the *prajñâ-pâramitâs*, the "higher perfections" developed by those who follow the *bodhisattva* path. This corrects the "spiritual materialism" inherent in the more popular Buddhist attitude toward doing good deeds, which is concerned with accumulating good *karma*. For Swedenborg too, those who are led by the Lord think of nothing less than the merit that their good works might accrue (*AC* 6392). His account of this would fit comfortably into a Mahâyâna scripture:

> When an angel [or *bodhisattva*!] does good to anyone he also communicates to him his own good, satisfaction, and blessedness; and this with the feeling that he would give to the other

everything, and retain nothing. When he is in such communication good flows into him with much greater satisfaction and blessedness than he gives, and this continually with increase. But as soon as a thought enters, that he will communicate his own to the intent that he may maintain that influx of satisfaction and blessedness into himself, the influx is dissipated; and still more if there comes in any thought of recompense from him to whom he communicates his good.   (*AC* 6478)

Unlike those who have retired from the world to live a solitary and devout life, an "angel's life is happy because of its blessedness and is made up of serving good purposes which are works of charity" (*HH* 535). Both traditions deny that salvation is effected by performing rituals, or faith alone, or deeds alone, or even by having mystical experiences. To be spiritual is to live a certain kind of life, in which love of self is replaced by selfless love.

In order to be able to live this way, we must be regenerated, which for Swedenborg involves an opening-up of our internals that seems very similar to the enlightenment or *parâvṛtti*, "turning around," of Buddhist liberation. The origin of evil is that "man turned himself backwards, away from the Lord, and round towards himself" (*CL* 444); we need to "turn back around" away from self and towards the Lord. This turning-around liberates the Lord's influx to flow into us. This influx is life itself. We have no other life of our own, being receptacles of this divine life. The question is how much of this influx we are open to. Depending on my ruling love, this influx is choked and constricted (by self-love) or flows like a fountain (into love of God and neighbor).

This points to the solution of a perennial religious problem: the relationship between personal effort and transcendental grace. This tension recurs in the argument between Augustine and Pelagius; in the Hindu Viśiṣṭadvaita debate about "cat salvation" (a mother cat carries her kittens) versus "monkey salvation" (a baby monkey must cling to its mother's chest); and in the Japanese Buddhist problem of the relationship between *tariki*, "other effort" (throwing oneself on the mercy of the Buddha), and *jiriki*, "self-effort" (which requires one's own efforts to become liberated). All "I" can do is to open up to the spiritual influx by my ego getting out of the way, that is, letting-go of myself, whereupon this influx necessarily fills me, just as the sun shines when the clouds dissipate. But this letting-go is rarely easy: insofar as the self is the problem, it is not something that the self can *do*. In Zen, for example, letting-go is not subject to my *willing*; during *zazen*, I learn how to "forget myself" indirectly, by concentrating on and becoming-one-with my meditation practice.[15]

Identification of the Divine

Although the issue is complicated, I think that Swedenborg's conception of the Divine avoids the extremes of a personal and impersonal Absolute in much the same way that Mahâyâna Buddhism does. The dilemma is that a completely impersonal Absolute, such as is found in certain types of Vedanta, must be indifferent to our situation; whereas a more personal God, understood to have a will and desires analogous to ours, may choose some people (or some peoples) for a special destiny—perhaps without their doing anything special to deserve it (e.g., predestination). Yet there is another alternative, if God is not other than us, if he is, in fact, the life-giving force in everything: our being, as Swedenborg might express it, or our lack of being, as Mahâyâna might express it—or both, as the thirteenth-century Christian mystic Meister Eckhart does express it, since both descriptions are ways to communicate the same insight, that there is no dualism between

God and us. So Eckhart can play with the binary terms "Being" and "Nonbeing" by nonchalantly reversing their meaning. Sometimes he refers to the being of creatures and describes God as a nothing, without the slightest bit of existence. At other times Eckhart contrasts the "nullity" of all creatures with the being of God, in which case it is not that God has being, or even that God is being, but that being is God *(esse est deus)*. If God is the life or being in everything, then it is just as true to say that nothing has any being of its own. Is this also an adequate explanation of the *śûnyatâ* (emptiness) of beings, according to Mahâyâna, and of the nature of the Lord for Swedenborg?

The nature of God and the role of Christ for Swedenborg are two difficult issues that are not fully addressed in *Heaven and Hell*; and even when we consider other writings that address those matters more fully—especially *Divine Love and Wisdom* and *Arcana Cœlestia*—I do not find what he writes entirely clear or satisfactory. Curiously, however, there is some of the same ambiguity within the Buddhist tradition. Let us consider the two issues separately.

For Swedenborg, God is life itself, of which angels and spirits and humans are recipients. This divine essence manifests as love and wisdom, which are inseparable in the same way as the sun's heat and light are—an inspired analogy or rather correspondence that Swedenborg makes much of, since in heaven God *appears as* (but is not himself) a sun (*HH* 116–140). When, however, we inquire into the nature of God in himself, apart from all the things infused and the activity of infusing them, what Swedenborg writes is less helpful. He emphasizes repeatedly that God is a man, or human. Three main reasons are given for this: humans, like angels and spirits, derive their form from God, "there being no difference as to form, but as to essence" (*AE* 1124; *DLW* 11);[16] heaven is in the form of a man, both in whole and in part (*HH* 59–72); and humans should conceive of God as a man, for it is not possible to think of, love, and be conjoined with something indefinite and therefore incomprehensible (e.g., *HH* 3; *TCR* 787; *AC* 8705, 7211, 9354).

What seems significant is that none of these reasons unambiguously implies *theism* as that term is usually understood. The first two do not require that God has a self-existence apart from his universe (in general) and from those beings who experience his influx (in particular); they imply something important about the form we and the universe necessarily embody as recipients of influx, yet nothing about the form-in-itself of the *source* of that influx. The third reason, the only one that offers an argument rather than an assertion, is more difficult to evaluate because it appears in several different versions; its general thrust, however, addresses *what we should think* rather than *what is the case*. Swedenborg is clearly concerned about the dangers of conceiving of God in the wrong way, insofar as this can lead us astray. Those who believe in an invisible Divine called the Reality of the Universe, the source of all that exists, end up believing in no divinity at all, because such a Divine "is no fit subject for thought" (*HH* 3); those who acknowledge what is incomprehensible "glide in thought into nature, and so believe in no God" (*AC* 9354). Yet, no one in heaven "can have any conception of the Divine in itself. . . . For the angels are finite and what is finite can have no conception of the infinite. In heaven, therefore, if they had not an idea of God in the human shape, they would have no idea, or an unbecoming one" (*AC* 7211).

In sum: inasmuch as God is infinite, all our conceptions of him must miss the mark, but inasmuch as we need a conception of him, the best image is that of a man. To a Buddhist, this is reminiscent of the old nineteenth-century argument that, since a religion must have a God, Buddhism cannot be a religion. The question this begs is: is it possible to have a religion (such as Buddhism) that criticizes *all* conceptions of the Divine, including the image of God as human, yet still functions as a religion because its spiritual practices nonetheless promote the divine influx?

Insofar as Swedenborg's quintessential teaching is that the Lord's love and wisdom flow into everything, then clearly no being exists apart from God, and the fact that God is human does not necessarily imply that God exists as human-like apart from beings. But this may be taken a step further. If we extrapolate from Swedenborg's favorite analogy—God as a formless, radiating sun—the Lord may be understood as a *potentiality* that achieves form only in his creation. From that perspective, *God needs us* in order to become fully real, both individually (as we open to his influx) and collectively (as his heaven grows and ramifies).

If this understanding is acceptable (and it may not have been to Swedenborg himself),[17] it is consistent with much of Buddhism and may even help to clarify some aspects of Buddhist teaching. Central to Mahâyâna is the concept of *śûnyatâ,* usually translated as "emptiness." For Nâgârjuna, the most important Mahâyâna philosopher, that things are *śûnya* is a shorthand way to express that no thing has any self-being or self-presence of its own. In the succinct *Heart Sutra,* a famous summary of the *prajñâpâramitâ* scriptures, the *bodhisattva* Avalokiteśvara realizes that "form is *śûnyatâ* and *śûnyatâ* is form; form is no other than *śûnyatâ* and *śûnyatâ is* no other than form." Unfortunately, the usual English translation "emptiness" does not convey the full connotations of the original, for the Sanskrit root *śû* literally means "swollen," not only like an inflated balloon but also like a pregnant woman *swollen with possibility.* According to Nâgârjuna, it is only because things are *śūnya* that any change, including spiritual development, is possible.

Śūnyatā, then, invites interpretation as a formless spiritual potential that is literally no-thing in itself yet functions as the "empty essence" that gives life to everything and enables it to be what it is. Such an influx is experienced as "empty" for two reasons: it has no particular form of its own/in itself, and insofar as I *am* it, I cannot *know* it. This is consistent with Swedenborg's understanding of the Lord as constituting the life in all of us, the heat and light that flow into us to the extent that we are receptive to it. On the Buddhist side, this also helps to avoid the nihilistic interpretation of *śūnyatā* that the rather-too-negative term has sometimes invited.

Śākyamuni Buddha, the historical founder of Buddhism who lived about five hundred years before Christ, did not urge his disciples to unite with God or experience his influx. Instead, he taught them to follow in his own footsteps by pursuing the same types of spiritual practice in order to attain the same *nirvāṇa*. However, this difference is less problematical than it might seem. For one thing, the nature of *nirvāṇa* is notoriously obscure, since the Buddha refused to say much about it except that it is the end of suffering and craving; those who want to know what *nirvāṇa* is must attain it for themselves. In addition, the comparative study of religion has led us to an insight that is difficult to deny today but would have had little meaning in Swedenborg's time: that very similar experiences may be subjected to different and incompatible explanations, according to the tradition one is familiar with. In Śākyamuni's time Indian popular religion was polytheistic, which means that he did not teach in the context of an absolute God transcending or incorporating all other gods; nor does he seem to have been familiar with the Upanishadic conception of an impersonal Brahman, another alternative being developed by other sages about the same time. So it is hardly surprising that Śâkyamuni did not communicate his own spiritual insight—the influx of love and wisdom that dissolved his ego-self—in either terms but instead created his own religious categories (no-self, *nirvâṇa*, etc.), unlike Swedenborg, who naturally understood his own experience in terms of the developed Christian tradition that he had grown up within, centered on the idea of an absolute Lord.

Later, and in different social contexts, theistic conceptions did become important in popular Buddhism, such as the Amida Buddha worshipped in more devotional sects of Buddhism. These devotional schools—which, as Swedenborg noticed, require that we think of the Divine as human—have undoubtedly been more important for more Buddhists than the dialectics of Buddhist philosophers such as Nâgârjuna.

In these ways Christian theism as Swedenborg explains it—the Lord as our life, due to his influx of love and wisdom—becomes more compatible with the *śûnyatâ* of Buddha-nature as many Buddhists have understood it.

Except for the unique role of Christ for Swedenborg. Here too, however, it seems to me that his understanding is not unproblematic. Taken as a whole, Swedenborg's writings contain a tension between two different positions that never quite become compatible. On the more orthodox side, he defends the uniqueness of Christ as God-Man and the importance of accepting him as our savior. On the other, more ecumenical side, his emphasis on the influx of love and wisdom leads him to reduce the salvific role of Christ so much that he can be reconceptualized without much difficulty as one *avatâr* among many, a view quite compatible with Buddhism.

Nevertheless, there is no doubt that Swedenborg understands the historical Christ as unique and the Christian church as special. Before Christ's advent, the Lord's influence was mediated through the angelic heavens, yet from the time God became human, it has been immediate. Since then the Christian church has formed the heart of the human race on earth and in heaven as well. Christians constitute the breast of the Grand Man, the center towards which all others look. It is not necessary that all or most people accept Christianity, but it is very important that some people do, "for from thence there is light to those who are out of the Church and have not the Word" (*DLW* 233; *AC* 637; *DP* 256).[18]

Yet who is in the Lord's spiritual church?

> [I]t is throughout the whole terrestrial globe. For it is not limited to those who have the Word, and from this have obtained a knowledge of the Lord, and some truths of faith; but it is also with those who have not the Word, and are therefore entirely ignorant of the Lord, and consequently do not know any truths of faith (for all truths of faith refer to the Lord); that is, with the Gentiles remote from the church. . . . And although ignorant of the Lord while in the world, yet they have within them the worship and tacit acknowledgement of Him, *when they are in good; for in good the Lord is present.* (*AC* 3263; my emphasis)

During his visits to hell Swedenborg encountered Church dignitaries learned in the Christian Word, "but in evils as to life," while in heaven he met both Christians and Gentiles "who were in falsities" and "were yet in good as to life" (*AC* 9192). When we are being regenerated, we can fight against falsities "even from truth not genuine if only it be such that it can be conjoined by any means with good; and it is conjoined with good by innocence, for innocence is the means of conjunction" (*AC* 6765). From passages such as these—and there are many of them—it is difficult to conclude that it is necessary or even important to be a Christian. The point is not simply that one is saved by living a good life, but that one lives a good life because one has become receptive to the influx of divine love and wisdom. And insofar as this influx is "innocent," it is unclear why it should be necessary to believe in any particular doctrine whatever. If we accept this important ecumenical strand within Swedenborg's writings, a strand that has been even more important in Buddhism, then there is no need for anyone to be a Christian or a Swedenborgian or a Buddhist, except insofar as those teachings and communities help us to turn away from self-love and open up to the influx of self-less love and wisdom.

Why did God manifest on earth as man? The internals of humans are under the dominion of either spirits from hell or angels from heaven; when in the course of time the hellish influence became stronger and "there was no longer any faith nor any charity," God's advent was necessary to restore order and redeem man (AC 152). This may be a good reason for the appearance of a savior, but it is a poor argument for the uniqueness of Christ as the savior. In fact, it is the same reason given in the *Bhagavad-Gîta* for the periodic appearance of *avatârs*, and in Buddhism for the periodic appearance of Buddhas (the one previous to Śâkyamuni was Dîpamkara; the next will be Maitreya).[19]

Spiritual Interdependence

In the previous section, the *śûnyatâ* "emptiness" of Mahâyâna Buddhism was interpreted as a formless spiritual potential that gives life to everything, an understanding that I have argued is consistent with Swedenborg's conception of God's influx into each of us. This approach to *śûnyatâ* has been especially important as a way to understand the *dharmakâya* ("Truth-body"), the highest reality according to Mahâyâna teachings, as we shall see shortly when we turn to the *Tibetan Book of the Dead*. However, this has not been the only understanding of *śûnyatâ* in Buddhism, and it is questionable whether it would have been acceptable to Nâgârjuna himself, who argued for the *śûnyatâ* of things not by referring to influx but by demonstrating interdependence (things are *śûnya* because they have no self-existence, being dependent on many other phenomena).

This emphasis on interdependence became an essential Mahâyâna teaching—in fact, *the* essential teaching of Hua-yen, a Chinese school of Buddhism that describes this relationship using the metaphor of Indra's Net:

> Far away in the heavenly abode of the great god Indra, there is a wonderful net that stretches out infinitely in all directions. . . . [There is] a single glittering jewel in each "eye" of the net, and since the net itself is infinite in all dimensions, the jewels are infinite in number. . . . [I]n its polished surface there are reflected all the other jewels in the net, infinite in number. Not only that, but each of the jewels reflected in this one jewel is also reflecting all the other jewels, so that there is an infinite reflecting process occurring.[20]

Indra's Net "thus symbolizes a cosmos in which there is an infinitely repeated interrelationship among all the members of the cosmos."[21] Each jewel is nothing other than a function of the relationships among all the others, and likewise may be said to contain all the others within itself. All is one and one is all: the whole world is contained in each thing, and each thing is nothing other than a manifestation of the whole world.

Is there anything comparable in Swedenborg? The analogy is hard to miss. All the realms of the heavens constitute a whole (*HH* 59–67)—in fact, a Grand Man—as does hell (*HH* 553); in that Grand Man who is heaven, for example, infants form the region of the eyes (*HH* 333). Each of heaven's communities is also a single person (*HH* 68–72), and conversely each angel is a heaven in smallest form (*HH* 53); the same relationship seems to hold for the hells and the demons in them.[22]

For Buddhism, however, there is a potential problem with this second conception of interdependence, which can understand the world as merely a mechanical relationship among material forces, something that is clearly not what Mâdhyamika and Hua-yen are wanting to describe. Understanding *śûnyatâ* as influx avoids this.

We end up with two different types of dependence: dependence of non-self-existent things on the influx of spiritual potentiality that gives them being/life, and the organic or "ecological" interdependence of each such thing on the functioning of all other things. What seems significant is that both types of dependence are important both to Mahâyâna and to Swedenborg. The interpenetration of one in all and all in one in Swedenborg's afterlife presupposes the divine influx that permeates all the realms, including hell where it is perverted into self-love. In Buddhism these two interpretations of *śûnyatâ* have often been antagonistic to each other, but Swedenborg's vision reminds us that they do not need to exclude each other.

This dependence/interdependence must be understood dynamically. Like Buddhism from its inception, Swedenborg emphasizes process (the Buddist *anitya*, impermanence) over substance *(svabhâva*, self-existence): persistence is a continual occurrence (*HH* 106), and enduring a constant emergence (*HH* 9). This is true even of Swedenborgian regeneration and Buddhist enlightenment. The regenerated are regenerated continually through life and also in the afterlife; heaven as it grows becomes more and more a Grand Man. Most Buddhist schools emphasize the need for continual practice, even for the deeply enlightened, and the urge to deepen one's practice endlessly is a sign of genuine realization. There is a saying in Zen that even Śâkyamuni Buddha is only halfway there.

Perhaps the clearest parallel of all is with Swedenborg's account of evil and its punishment, which is so Buddhist in spirit that it could be used to explain the Buddhist doctrines of *karma* and *saṃskâra*; again, Swedenborg's explanation perhaps helps to clarify the Buddhist perspective. Like Śâkyamuni Buddha and, for that matter, Christ himself, Swedenborg emphasizes intention (e.g., *HH* 508). In this way evil becomes tied to its own punishment:

> Every evil carries its punishment with it, the two making one; therefore whoever is in evil is also in the punishment of evil. And yet no one in the other world suffers punishment on account of the evils that he had done in this world, but only on account of the evils that he then does; although it amounts to the same and is the same thing whether it be said that people suffer punishment on account of their evils in the world or that they suffer punishment on account of the evils they do in the other life, since every one after death returns into his own life and thus into like evils; and the person continues the same as he had been in the life of the body. . . . But good spirits, although they had done evils in the world, are never punished, because their evils do not return.   (*HH* 509)

> The Lord does not do evil to anyone.   (*HH* 550)

> Evil has its own punishment, thus hell, goodness its own reward, thus heaven.   (*AC* 9033)

This is, in effect, a sophisticated account of *karma* that avoids both the problem with a more mechanical understanding of moral cause-and-effect (common in popular Buddhism) and the problem with a more juridical understanding of hell as punishment for disobeying divine authority (common in popular Christianity). Swedenborg's central insight is that people suffer or are rewarded not for what they have done but for what they have become, and *what we intentionally do is what makes us what we are.* That is why, in most cases, there is no difference between the evil things done in the world and the evil things that one is inclined to do in the afterworld. This conflation makes no sense if *karma* is understood dualistically as a kind of moral dirt obscuring one's mirror-like pure self. It makes a great deal of sense if I *am* my intention or ruling love, for then the important spiritual issue is the development of that ruling love. In the latter case, my actions and my intentions build my character—that is, my spiritual body—just as surely as food is assimilated to become my physical body.

All schools of Buddhism similarly emphasize the importance of our *saṃskâras*, which are mental tendencies: one's habitual ways of intending and reacting to particular situations. In Buddhism, too, these *saṃskâras* are the vehicles of *karma.* They survive death and cause rebirth; in fact, they are what is reborn, since there is no pure self to be reincarnated. And how are such mental tendencies formed?

> We can now see that it is not so hard to lead a heaven-bound life as people think it is because it is simply a matter, when something gets in the way that people know is dishonest and unfair, something the spirit moves toward, of thinking that they should not do it because it is against divine precepts. If we get used to doing this, and by getting used to it gain a certain disposition, then little by little we are bonded to heaven. As this takes place, the higher reaches of the mind are opened; and as they are opened, we see things that are dishonest and unfair; and as we see things as they are, they can be broken apart. . . .
>
> But it must be understood that the difficulty of so thinking and of resisting evils increases so far as man from his will does evils, for in the same measure he becomes accustomed to them until he no longer sees them, and at length loves them and from the delight of his love excuses them, and confirms them

by every kind of fallacy, and declares them to be allowable and good. *(HH 533)*

A person suffers not because of "inherited evil" but "because of the realized evil that does belong to him—that is, the amount of inherited evil that he has made his own by his life activities" *(HH 342)*. In this way Swedenborg and Buddhism both present a psychological version of *karma* that denies any sharp distinction between the one who intends and the intention itself. I *am* my predominant intentions, which means that habitually acting in certain ways is what *constructs* me. That is why a person with bad *saṃskâras*—a "bad character"— cannot be saved in spite of himself: because he *is* those *saṃskâras,* which cannot dwell in heaven because they would not be comfortable there. Therefore, they spontaneously go to where they are comfortable, which happens to be where there are others with similar *saṃskâras.* One of the reasons evil people suffer in the afterworld is the same reason good people are blessed there: they end up living with others just like them.

The Spirit World

Swedenborg's account of the world of spirits (part two of *HH*) has many similarities with the Tibetan understanding of the afterlife and the rebirth process, which provides by far the most detailed account among the various Buddhist traditions. However, there are some problems in working this out. The *Bardo Thödol Chenmo* text, first translated by W. Y. Evans-Wentz and published as *The Tibetan Book of the Dead,* is only one of several such *Bardo* texts in the Tibetan tradition; and because that particular text was composed with reference to a tantric mandala of 110 peaceful and wrathful deities, there is much obscure symbolism about those deities.[23]

Yet even if one ignores this difficult iconography—to which I will return later—there remains a sophisticated description of death, intermediate life, and rebirth that resonates deeply with Swedenborg's account. Both emphasize the importance of one's last thought (*HH* 444)—in other words, the particular *saṃskâra* activated at the moment of death—and that all one's *saṃskâras* survive death, along with a psychic body that duplicates one's physical body: "after death, man is possessed of every sense, and of all the memory, thought, and affection that he had in the world, leaving behind nothing except his earthly body" (*HH*, title of chapter 48). Even as God does not turn his face from anyone and does not cast anyone into hell (*HH* 545), so the luminosity of the *dharmakâya* (experienced as a primordial clear light comparable to the divine sun in Swedenborg's heaven), which is nothing other than one's own *śûnyatâ* mind, does not reject anyone. For both there is a self-judgment that occurs in the presence of God/the *dharmakâya*, in which the true nature of one's *saṃskâras*/ruling affections becomes revealed to oneself. In the *Bardo* tradition, too, the good and wise are attracted to the pure, formless *dharmakâya*, and the texts urge them to become one with it; yet since it mirrors all one's *karma*, those less good are repulsed by it and are attracted to the *saṃsâric* realm that corresponds to their ruling *karma*.

Swedenborg emphasizes the limits of the Lord's mercy: no one enters heaven by direct mercy (*HH* 521–527), for the Lord does not and evidently cannot violate the design that he *is* (*HH* 523). Since this mercy is constant with each individual and never withdraws, everyone who can be saved is saved; but those whose ruling affection is evil have learned to shut out his influx. In the intermediate *Bardo* realm, too, even a Buddha cannot stop someone who wants to go somewhere, since (as Swedenborg expresses it) he or she is that attraction/affection and could not be stopped without being annihilated (*HH* 527).

There are, nevertheless, some important differences. For Swedenborg the world of spirits is an intermediate one because there one is "devastated": that is, outward elements must be changed until they conform with inward elements (*HH* 426). One's inmost level can no longer be reformed, but the outward elements must be gradually set in order until one's ways of thinking and feeling are consistent with one's deepest intentions. Yet, as the meaning of the Tibetan title ("The Great Liberation through Hearing in the Bardo") suggests, the presupposition of the *Bardo* ("intermediate realm") texts is that it is still possible to exercise some freedom in the *Bardo* world, that despite the *karmic* attraction there may still be some choice in the matter—perhaps because there may be more than one "ruling" love. I can think of two ways to resolve this difference. One is to understand the *Bardo Thödol* less ingenuously as a book meant for the living rather than the dead, as a way of encouraging the survivors to reform their lives—their *saṃskâras*—while they still can. Reading it orally beside the corpse, surrounded by the chastened mourners, certainly serves this function, yet there is another way to look at it. I wonder if there is some inconsistency in the way that *Heaven and Hell* emphasizes that one's ruling love cannot be changed to eternity (*HH* 477ff.), while also describing incidents such as angels' attempts to influence new spirits (e.g., *HH* 450), which efforts would be largely wasted if they could have no effect whatsoever on one's ruling love (and therefore one's eventual place in heaven or hell). It also seems debatable whether we always have only *one* ruling love; maybe there are some cases, or many cases, where two or more affections contend with each other throughout one's life and even afterwards. Perhaps Swedenborg's book is the disingenuous one.

A difference of emphasis, or more, follows from the distinction between morality and insight. They are closely related, yet to the extent that they may be distinguished, Buddhism as a "wisdom tradition" emphasizes wisdom more, while Swedenborg emphasizes morality. One of the ways this difference shows itself is in the distinction that Buddhism makes between "heaven" as one of the six realms of *saṁsâra*—pleasurable yet complacent, therefore not as good a place to be as our present human realm—and the liberation that is *nirvâṇa*. From a Buddhist perspective, even good *karma* is troublesome insofar as it operates mechanically; better is the *prajñâ* wisdom that frees one from all *karma* and, therefore, from all the realms of *saṁsâra*. A good example of this is the *Bardo Thödol* understanding of what happens after death when a new spirit encounters the pure luminosity of the *dharmakâya*. One is encouraged to unite with the white light by realizing that one *is* it; in comparison to this, even the most sublime of the peaceful deities, which represent good *karma*, is nothing more than a higher form of delusion. I do not find this distinction in Swedenborg.

This leads us to consider the most important difference between Swedenborg and Buddhism, and what is undoubtedly a major obstacle to any conflation. Swedenborg's Christian conception of the afterdeath drama is orthodox in understanding this life as a one-chance preparation for heaven or hell, since one's ruling love never changes, even to eternity (*HH* 477, 480). In contrast, all traditional schools of Buddhism understand the alternative to *nirvâṇa* as rebirth in one of the six *saṁsâric* realms (heaven, titan, human, hungry ghost, animal, and hell), which includes the possibility of returning as a human being.[24] However, even this difference is complicated by the fact that some *Bardo Thödol* passages warn the spirit about never being able to escape from where one is inclined to go: "now is the time when by slipping into laziness even for a moment you will suffer forever." "If you go there you will enter hell and experience unbearable suffering through heat and cold from which you will never get out."[25] Theoretically, though, escape is always possible no matter where you are, if you realize the *śûnyatâ* of your own mind. The corresponding experience in Swedenborg would be regeneration even in hell, by the opening up of one's internals to the Lord's influx and the transformation of one's ruling love; yet he does not allow for that possibility, despite the fact that divine love never withdraws from anyone (*DP* 330).

Living Correspondences

As a final comparison, let us briefly consider Swedenborg's doctrine of correspondences and representations, which constitutes a version of afterlife idealism: although the afterworld is in many ways similar to this one, things there are not as fixed or stationary, for their condition varies according to the angels that perceive them, and they disappear when those angels depart (*HH* 173ff.):

> As all things that correspond to interiors also represent them they are called representations; and as they differ in each case in accordance with the state of the interiors they are called appearances. Nevertheless, the things that appear before the eyes of angels in heaven and are perceived by their senses appear to their eyes and senses as fully living as things on earth appear to man, and even much more clearly, distinctly and perceptibly.
>
> (*HH* 175)

To any Buddhist philosopher this sounds very similar to the Buddhist school known as Yogâcâra or Vijñânavâda (sometimes translated as "the Representation-only School"). This is the other important philosophical school of Mahâyâna, along with Nâgârjuna's Mâdhyamika, with which it eventually merged. In contrast to the detailed correspondences offered by

Swedenborg, Yogâcâra addresses the issue on a more abstract level which, frankly, I have not found very interesting. More illuminating is the parallel with the *Bardo Thödol*, which understands all postmortem experiences as mentally-projected images, making the world beyond "a *karmically* corresponding image of earthly life":

> The descriptions of those visions which, according to the *Bardo Thödol,* appear in the intermediate state *(bar-do)* following death are neither primitive folklore nor theological speculations. They are not concerned with the appearances of supernatural beings . . . but with the visible projections or reflexes of inner processes, experiences, and states of mind, produced in the creative phase of meditation.[26]

The challenge of the Bardo realm is to recognize the peaceful and wrathful deities that appear as the karmic projections of one's own mind. "If all the temptations of deceptive visionary images, which are constantly referred to in the texts as hostile forms of the intellect, can be recognized as empty creations of one's own mind and can be immediately penetrated, one will attain liberation."[27]

The difference, as we have already noted, is that the *Bardo Thödol* urges the deceased not to identify with any such images in order to attain to the liberating luminosity of the *dharmakâya*, while Swedenborg's angels dwell happily in a mental world that changes constantly according to their affections. Perhaps the common ground between them is that neither spirit is deceived by those correspondences into believing that the things of one's world are real, a delusion that occurs when *samsâric* attachments and delusions motivate us to fixate on them. One who *must* play cannot *play*, while those who know things are correspondences are not trapped by and in those correspondences.

If the above parallels are genuine, they raise a concluding question that should not be ignored: why are Buddhist and Swedenborg's teachings so similar in these ways? There are various possibilities, which readers can work out for themselves; but one ramification in particular deserves to be addressed: did Swedenborg become acquainted with Buddhism through his travels in the afterworld? One of the most intriguing references in his voluminous works is an allusion to "Great Tartary" where the teachings of the Ancient Church have been preserved:

> I have spoken with spirits and angels who came from there, and they said that they possess a Word, and have from ancient times; and that their divine worship is performed according to this Word, *which consists of pure correspondences.* . . . They said that they worship Jehovah, some as an invisible, and some as a visible God. Moreover they said that they do not permit foreigners to come among them, except the Chinese, with whom they cultivate peace, because the emperor of China is from their country. . . . Seek for it in China, and perhaps you will find it there among the Tartars. (*AR* 11; my emphasis)[28]

What does this refer to? And where? Anders Hallengren discusses this matter in his article "The Secret of Great Tartary."[29] After reviewing the historical evidence, he concludes that the most probable reference is the Buddhism of Mongolia and Tibet (since Kublai Khan, founder of the Chinese Yuan dynasty, was converted by a Tibetan *rinpoche* in the thirteenth century, Mongolian Buddhism has been a version of Tibetan Buddhism). To this I can add only one point, concerning the curious fact that their worship "consists of pure correspondences." What can this mean? The Vajrayâna Buddhism of

Tibet and Mongolia is a Mahâyâna form of *tantra* that employs meditative practices such as *maṇḍalas* (complex visual images, usually paintings), *mantras* (the repetition of sacred sounds), *mudrâs* (hand movements), and so forth. In the case of a *maṇḍala,* for example, a practitioner typically meditates on its visual form until he or she is able to reproduce it completely—indeed, it is said to be clearer—in the mind's eye; finally one unites with the deities depicted, who represent aspects of one's own Buddha-nature. The complex symbolism of most *maṇḍalas* is not very relevant to the theoretical concerns of most Buddhist philosophers, while the opposite is true for meditators. *Tantra* is by nature esoteric because it is a nonconceptual symbolic system: "the mandala is a microcosmic image of the universe;"[30] it "is, above all, a map of the cosmos. It is the whole universe in its essential plan, in its process of emanation and reabsorption."[31] This suggests that meditations employing these images might be the pure correspondence that Swedenborg mentions. I do not know how to evaluate this supposition, but in the future I will be less inclined to dismiss such images as "mere iconography."

Conclusion

Here it has been possible to mention only some of the more provocative parallels between Swedenborgianism and Buddhism. It has, nevertheless, been enough to suggest that Swedenborg could serve as an important bridge in the contemporary dialogue between Christianity and Buddhism. Swedenborg's double emphasis on divine love and wisdom, which forms the core of his theology, is reproduced in the relationship between Christianity and Buddhism, which respectively emphasize the way of love and the way of wisdom—and, as Swedenborg and Buddhism both emphasize, each way entails the other. I also hope to have shown how Swedenborg and Buddhism can illuminate each other. In particular, Buddhism, with probably the world's richest collection of meditative techniques and practices, has much to offer those Swedenborgians who seek more specific guidance on how to "let go" of themselves in order to realize personally the spiritual influx that Swedenborg's grand metaphysical system describes so well.

Unfortunately, we cannot expect this bridge to carry much traffic, for the same reason that Swedenborg's eschatology has been ignored by the mainstream Christian tradition: his grand conception of the afterworld, and of this world, is too dependent on his own extraordinary spiritual experiences, which few if any of us seem able to confirm for ourselves.

Not having visited heaven or hell, I can only hope that, if they exist, they function in the way Swedenborg has described. After one studies his remarkably detailed yet well-structured eschatology, others begin to lose their credibility. This response is itself a remarkable fact, pointing to the utter plausibility of this grandest of narratives. If the universe doesn't function in the way Swedenborg explained, well, it should.[32]

Notes

1. *Tricycle: The Buddhist Review* (Fall 1991): 6–7.

2. George Dole, Review of *How the Swans Came to the Lake,* *Chrysalis* 9, no. 1 (Spring 1994): 75.

3. Philangi Dasa, *Swedenborg the Buddhist, or The Higher Swedenborgianism, Its Secrets and Thibetan* Origin (Los Angeles: The Buddhistic Swedenborgian Brotherhood, 1887), 14. I am grateful to Leonard Fox for providing me with a photocopy of this book.

4. Did Suzuki read *The Buddhist Ray* while he was working for the Open Court Publishing Company? It is likely that Paul Carus was aware of it.

5. Mihoko Bekku, personal communication. Yukie Dan, secretary of the Eastern Buddhist Society (which publishes *The Eastern Buddhist*, a journal founded by Suzuki), has provided me with a list of Swedenborg references in Suzuki's collected writings (in Japanese): a total of ten, in addition to the studies and translations already mentioned. "Generally, Swedenborg is not thought to be of much importance to Suzuki, who does not mention him overtly. But this information sheet, listing fairly explicit mentions of ES, would suggest that Swedenborg was never apart from Suzuki. So we now believe he is significant, but significant in which way has yet to be elucidated." (Yukie Dan, personal communication.)

6. Contact between India and Europe occurred long before Alexander's conquests (326–323 B.C.), and Marco Polo gives an account of the legend of the Buddha. In the thirteenth century papal envoys visited the Mongol Khan, and their accounts aroused much interest in Europe. Later missionaries also sent back numerous reports; but since few of these were published, it is difficult to determine how much correct information on Buddhism reached Europe before the nineteenth century. The important exception, curiously, was Tibet. At the end of the sixteenth century, Jesuit missionaries believed that Christians lived there, and a series of Catholic missionaries visited, beginning in 1624. One of them, Ippolito Desideri, stayed in Lhasa for five years (1716–1721) and acquired an excellent knowledge of Tibetan language and religion; he wrote a "Relazione" on his studies during his return but this was not published until 1904. Only in the nineteenth century did systematic studies of Buddhism begin and reliable translations begin to appear. See J.W. De Jong, *A Brief History of Buddhist Studies in Europe and America* (Delhi, India: Sri Satguru Publications, 1987), 5–15.

7. See Emanuel Swedenborg, *Heaven and Its Wonders and Hell*, trans. George F. Dole (New York: Swedenborg Foundation, 1976), hereinafter referred to as *HH*. In the Swedenborgian tradition, numbers following a title's abbreviation refer to the numbered paragraphs in each work, not to page numbers.

8. As quoted in Philip Kapleau, ed., *The Three Pillars of Zen* (Tokyo: Weatherhill, 1965), 205. The original reference is from the Sokushin-zebutsu fascicle of Dôgen's *Shôbôgenzô*, but the same point is made by Dôgen in other fascicles as well.

9. See also *HH* 145. While the spiritual importance of the forehead and the top of the head (the parietal aperture left by the
fontanelle) has been largely ignored in the Christian tradition, it has
been emphasized in the Buddhist tantric and Indian yogic traditions,
which have a system of seven *chakras* that puts greatest importance
on the "third eye" in the middle of the forehead and the *chakra* at
the top of the head (according to the Tibetan tradition, the latter
chakra is the best way for the mental body to exit the physical body
after death).

10. In "*Genjô-kôan,*" the first and most important *Shôbôgenzô*
fascicle, as translated in *Moon in a Dewdrop: Writings of Zen Master Dôgen,* ed. Kazuaki Tanahashi (San Francisco: North Point Press,
1985), 70.

11. Emanuel Swedenborg, *Spiritual Diary,* five volumes, trans.
and ed. George Bush, John H. Smithson, and James Buss (London:
James Speirs, 1883–1902), hereinafter referred to as *SD.*

12. Emanuel Swedenborg, *Divine Love and Wisdom,* trans. John
C. Ager, 2nd edition (West Chester, PA: Swedenborg Foundation,
1995), hereinafter referred to as *DLW.*

13. Emanuel Swedenborg, *Marital Love and Its Wise Delights,*
trans. William F. Wunsch (New York: Swedenborg Foundation,
1856). This work also is called *Conjugial Love* and will be referred
to in the text as *CL.*

14. Emanuel Swedenborg, *Arcana Coelestia,* trans. John F. Potts
(New York: Swedenborg Foundation, 1837), hereinafter referred to
as *AC.*

15. Swedenborg says little about meditation practices, although
True Christian Religion 767 mentions the Lord appearing as a sun
before angels when they practice spiritual meditation. Swedenborg's
own preferred practice was meditating on the meaning of the Bible
and allowing his mind to be guided by the Lord into an awareness of
its spiritual significance. He also practiced breathing exercises,
which Suzuki discusses in his study. See Emanuel Swedenborg, *True
Christian Religion,* trans. John C. Ager (New York: Swedenborg
Foundation, 1898), hereinafter referred to as *TCR.*

16. See Emanuel Swedenborg, *Apocalypse Explained,* trans. John
C. Ager, rvd. John Whitehead (New York: Swedenborg Foundation,
1896), hereinafter referred to as *AE.*

17. *TCR* 19–20 emphasises that God is both substance itself and form itself (each of which requires the other) and that the substances and forms of both angels and humans are derived from God.

18. See Emanuel Swedenborg, *Divine Providence*, trans. William F. Wunsch, 2nd edition (West Chester, PA: Swedenborg Foundation 1996), hereinafter referred to as *DP*.

19. Krishna: "Whenever there is a decline in righteousness and rise of unrighteousness, then I send forth [incarnate] Myself. For the protection of the good, for the destruction of the wicked, and for the establishment of righteousness, I come into being from age to age" (*Gîta* 4:7–8).

20. Francis H. Cook, *Hua-yen Buddhism: The Jewel Net of Indra* (University Park, PA: Pennsylvania State University Press, 1977), 2.

21. Ibid.

22. Much of Swedenborg's vision of the afterworld, and this aspect in particular, is compatible with John Hick's concluding theory in *Death and Eternal Life* (London: Collins, 1976), an almost exhaustive historical study of Christian eschatology that, characteristically of modern theology, ignores Swedenborg's. "The distinction between the self as ego and the self as person suggests that as the human individual becomes perfected he becomes more and more a person and less and less an ego. Since personality is essentially outward-looking, as a relationship to other persons, whilst the ego forms a boundary limiting true personal life, the perfected individual will have become a personality without egoity, a living consciousness which is transparent to the other consciousnesses in relation to which it lives in a full community of love. Thus we have the picture of a plurality of personal centres without separate peripheries. They will have ceased to be mutually exclusive and will have become mutually inclusive and open to one another in a richly complex shared consciousness. The barrier between their common unconscious life and their individual consciousnesses will have disappeared, so that they experience an intimacy of personal community which we can at present barely imagine" (Hicks, 459–60).

Not a bad description of Swedenborg's heaven; compare *AC* 2057: "Mutual love in heaven consists in this, that they love the neighbor more than themselves. Hence the whole heaven presents as it were a single man; for they are all thus consociated by mutual love from the Lord. Hence it is that the happinesses of all are communicated to each, and those of each to all. The heavenly form is therefore such that every one is as it were a kind of center; thus a center of communication and therefore of happiness from all; and this according to all the diversities of that love, which are innumerable."

23. On the *Bardo Thödol,* see Glenn H. Mullin, *Death and Dying: The Tibetan Tradition* (London: Arkana, 1986), 21–22.

24. *HH* 256 gives an alternative explanation for the belief that people "can return to a former life": occasionally a confused "recollection" can occur due to experiencing the memories of spirits that always accompany us.

25. *The Tibetan Book of the Dead,* trans. with commentary by Francesca Fremantle and Chögyam Trungpa (Boston: Shambhala, 1992), 199; 212–213.

26. Lama Anagarika Govinda, *Foundations of Tibetan Mysticism* (New York: Samuel Weiser, 1969), 122.

27. Detlef Ingo Lauf, *Secret Doctrines of the Tibetan Book of the Dead* (Boston: Shambhala, 1989), 69.

28. See also *CL* 77; *The Coronis* 39 (found in Emanuel Swedenborg, *Posthumous Theological Works,* vol. 1, trans. John Whitehead, 2nd edition [West Chester, PA: Swedenborg Foundation, 1996]); and *SD* 6077.

29. *Arcana* 1, no. 1 (Fall 1994): 35–54.

30. Lauf, *Secret Doctrines,* 65.

31. Giuseppe Tucci, *The Theory and Practice of the Mandala* (London: Rider and Co., 1969), 23.

32. I am grateful to many Swedenborgian scholars, especially Leonard Fox, Donald Rose, Dan Synnestvedt, Erik E. Sandström, and Jane Williams-Hogan, for their comments on earlier drafts of this paper.

Index

About the Contributors

Daisetsu Teitarô Suzuki (1870–1966) is credited with introducing the West to Zen Buddhism. Suzuki pursued his religious and philosophical studies at Tokyo University. After a ten-year sojourn in the United States, where he worked as an editor of Oriental Studies for Open Court Press, Suzuki returned to his native Japan where he undertook the translation of Swedenborg's works into Japanese. Throughout his long life, this Buddhist scholar taught at colleges in Japan, the United States, and Europe, including Columbia, Yale, Harvard, Cambridge, and Oxford. His works are collected in the 32-volume *Suzuki Daisetsu Zenshû* (Tokyo: 1968). Among his works available in English are *Essays in Zen Buddhism, Mysticism: Christian and Buddhist*, and *Zen and Japanese Culture*.

Andrew Bernstein received his B.A. from Amherst College and his M.A. in religion from Columbia University, where he is currently working toward his Ph.D. Between college and graduate school, he spent several years in Tokyo as a journalist. He plans to return to Japan to do research for his dissertation on the relationship between Buddhism and Japanese intellectuals in the early twentieth century.

David Loy, a professor in the Faculty of International Studies, Bunkyo University, Japan, has published widely in the field of comparative philosophy and religion. His books include *Nonduality: A Study in Comparative Philosophy* (1988) and *Lack and Transcendence: Death and Life in Psychotherapy, Existentialism and Buddhism* (1996). A student of Zen for many years, he is qualified as a *sensei* (teacher) in the Sanbo Kyodan lineage. He lives with his wife and son in Kamakura, the historic old capital of Japan.

Tatsuya Nagashima received his B.A. in Latin and his M.A. in philosophy from Sophia University in Tokyo; he also holds a B.Th. from Seinan Gakuin University in Fukuoka. He translated the *Nuntium Apostolorum* into Japanese. He is currently a professor at Shikoku University in Tokushima, Japan; and manager of the Arcana Press, which published the first Japanese translations of Swedenborg's writings from the original Latin.